Praise for *Eve*

Suffering? Who has n̲ ̲ ̲ ̲ ̲ ̲ ̲ ̲ ̲ ̲ ̲ ̲ ̲. The loss of a loved one. The loss of health. The loss of possessions. No one is exempt from some form of malady or pain. No wonder then that we ask if things happen for a reason or if things occur only by happenstance. Enns addresses this issue in a most thorough way. If we suffer, how can God be sovereign? Or if God is loving, why doesn't He do something about our problems? This book will be a source of great comfort for anyone who asks, "Does everything happen for a reason?"

—DR. ROY B. ZUCK, Senior Professor Emeritus of Bible Exposition at Dallas Theological Seminary, and editor, *Bibliotheca Sacra*

If we are honest, we all struggle to understand what God may be up to in those hard, tragic, and confusing times of loss and suffering. Paul Enns brings a clarity to the question of "Why God?" in this insightful, personal, and encouraging book. *Everything Happens for a Reason?* brings what many persecuted Christians know about God's special closeness during suffering into clear focus for us—it will enlighten and encourage you.

—DR. CARL MOELLER, President/CEO, Open Doors USA

When my wife, Barbara, and I lost our four-and-a-half year old daughter, Nancy, we felt numb and powerless, but we knew that God would carry us through. When we each accepted Jesus Christ as our Lord and Savior, our lives were never again the same. Paul Enns' book elucidates poignantly the sovereignty of God and his promise "to carry us through." Even in our suffering, God is in control. Barbara and I found the cure in the glory of God's hope. As Paul Enns reiterates in the message of James 1:3, "the testing of our faith produces endurance," our suffering invites a closer relationship with God, and this is our triumph. Thank you for sharing your story and the hope found only in the grace of our Almighty Father.

—**SAM RUTIGLIANO**, former head coach of the
NFL's Cleveland Browns

EVERYTHING
HAPPENS
FOR A REASON?

God's Purposes in a World Gone Bad

PAUL ENNS

MOODY PUBLISHERS
CHICAGO

© 2012 by
PAUL ENNS

Edited by Jim Vincent
Interior design: Ragont Design
Cover design: Connie Gabbert Design and Illustration, LLC
Cover image: millennium images (millim.com) / z600_281

Library of Congress Cataloging-in-Publication Data

Enns, Paul P., 1937-
Everything happens for a reason? : God's purposes in a world gone bad / Paul Enns.
    p. cm.
Includes bibliographical references.
ISBN 978-0-8024-0598-2
1. Providence and government of God--Christianity. 2. Theodicy. 3. Suffering--Religious aspects--Christianity. I. Title.
 BT135.E56 2012
 231'.8--dc23
                          2012004951

We hope you enjoy this book from Moody Publishers. Our goal is to provide high-quality, thought provoking books and products that connect truth to your real needs and challenges. For more information on other books and products written and produced from a biblical perspective, go to
www.moodypublishers.com
or write to:

Moody Publishers
820 N. LaSalle Boulevard
Chicago, IL 60610

1 3 5 7 9 10 8 6 4 2

Printed in the United States of America

To the Ennses, the Schroeders,
the Klassens, and the Paetkaus,
and to our other Mennonite and Anabaptist ancestors
who suffered for their faith

Contents

1

Why Do Bad Things Happen?

Just a decade ago, on a blue-sky morning with most workers in their offices in downtown New York City, a U.S. jetliner crashed into the north tower of the World Trade Center, some twenty stories from the top. Eighteen minutes later, another commercial jet slammed into the south tower, engulfing the upper floors in a gigantic ball of fire. Americans were stunned to learn that both planes had been hijacked by Arab Muslim extremists.

Billowing clouds of gray smoke churned across the ground surrounding the twin towers, and debris cascaded from above. Screaming in terror, people fled from the buildings, streaming into the streets as they ran to save their lives. Desperate and unable to escape the inferno, some people jumped to their deaths on the pavement below. One couple held hands as they jumped from the building.

STREETS STAINED WITH BLOOD

The graphic pictures of men and women fleeing the billowing smoke in terror, others disoriented, bloodied, and covered with soot, will forever remain etched in the minds of television viewers. A mountain of mangled steel . . . body parts lying in the rubble . . . streets stained with blood. It was an unparalleled criminal act and tragedy.

About an hour after the assault on the World Trade Center, a third plane, also commandeered by hijackers, plunged into the Pentagon, killing all sixty-four passengers and six crew members, and at least 189 military personnel at the Pentagon. Terrorists had penetrated to the very heart of America, Washington, D.C. If America's capital isn't safe, what is safe? The terrorists achieved their goal of striking terror into the hearts of many.

A fourth hijacked plane, apparently intended for a strike on the White House and the president himself, crashed into a field one hundred miles from Pittsburgh, killing all on board. Brave passengers apparently had fought the hijackers; the plane dove wildly to the ground, but these heroes saved the nation from further grief by diverting the plane from Washington.

THE WHY QUESTION

Thousands were killed in these four criminal, terrorist acts. Yet each death represented an individual story: A missing husband . . . a mother gone . . . a father lost . . . a brother searching for his brother . . . a son, a daughter beginning a career . . . now gone. Unquestionably, many believers were killed in the devastation. Some believing father, mother died that day. Why did it happen?

Why do tragedies happen to Christians? Why were Christians included in this carnage? Why do bad things happen to God's people?

GRANDMOTHER'S STORY

We will seek answers to those questions in this book. But let's remember that most personal sufferings are not found at scenes of war or national emergencies. Unseen, unknown, in the quiet corners of homes and hospitals, many Christians suffer tragedy and heartache.

Even though I was only a young boy, I remember my grandmother well. She was the picture of peacefulness and tranquility. She would sit by the window, the Bible on her lap, watching the activity outside; she would play checkers or other little games with her grandchildren. But perhaps the thing I remember most about her was her uncomplaining spirit. I never heard her speak a negative word; harsh, critical words were not part of her vocabulary or thoughts. On the contrary, she was thankful for the smallest things, for the proverbial "cup of water."

The grace of God and the peace of Christ enveloped her life; she had discovered the secret of submission to the sovereign will of God, and she lived in quiet assurance because of it. Her submission impressed me most because of all the pain and loss she had endured.

Humanly speaking, many bad things had happened to Oma. She was born in a Mennonite home and community in the Ukraine, near the Dnieper River. Because of religious persecution, her parents had migrated to the Ukraine from Prussia. There the persecution that her family had experienced would continue. When the communist revolution occurred in 1917, many Mennonites were brutally murdered and their farms confiscated.

During those tragic, bloody years, my grandmother buried two husbands and nine of her ten children. Life was difficult and bad things happened to good, God-fearing people. Typhoid fever, epidemics, murder—there were many causes for the suffering and death of the Mennonite families in addition to the brutalities caused by the communists. As I researched the family history, I was astonished to discover the untimely deaths of my grandmother's children: Jacob the first, age ten; Peter, age thirty-one; David, age unrecorded; Johan, age one; Aganetha, age unrecorded; Anna the first, age one; Anna the second, age two; Jacob the second, age twenty; Isaak the first, infant.

My mind reeled. How could my grandmother cope with

tragedy after tragedy in her family? Why were these bad things happening to her?

In 1927, after living under Communism for ten frightening years, she was able to emigrate to western Canada with my parents. Oma settled in Morris, Manitoba, with her last remaining child, my father, and with his family.

Oma loved her family, and her love overflowed to the grandchildren. She interceded for them when they were going to be disciplined and wept for them when they were disciplined—and quietly slipped them a cookie or candy to soften the suffering. But all the while Oma had her own continuing adversity. Despite being in a land of peace and plenty, she suffered physically. My grandmother had an enlarged, ulcerated foot that refused to heal. I still remember the putrid smell of the sore. But never a complaint. Oma had discovered a simple trust in the sovereign plan of God— despite not understanding why bad things happen to God's people.

WHY DID GRANDMOTHER BURY NINE CHILDREN?

Grandmother's life, like the New York and Washington tragedies, raises a fundamental question: Why do bad things happen to God's people? Why did my grandmother bury two husbands and nine children? Why was she forced to flee from her home and adopted country? Why did she suffer with an ailment that refused to heal? She was a God-fearing believer. Why did believers die in the destruction of the World Trade Center and in the attack on the Pentagon? Where was God in all of this? Is He in control?

Does the Bible explain why bad things happen to God's people? As a pastor I visit people in the hospitals—Christians who have terminal cancer, heart attacks, limb amputations . . . the list is endless. How do we explain the tragedies of life that Christians experience? Is God in control over the bad things that happen to God's people . . . or are the tragic events of this world simply blind, chance happenings?

Some say, "Everything happens for a reason." Does it? Rather than be hopeful or fatalistic, let's go to the ultimate source of truth and assurance, the Bible, to answer the question. God's Word has much to say about tragedy, loss, and suffering. Join me as we address the question, "Does everything happen for a reason?"

2

How Did Bad Things Begin?

It's difficult to believe the statement "Everything happens for a reason," because so much that happens seems to be based on bad situations or even people who behave badly.

The story behind the terrorist attacks on American landmarks on September 11, 2001, a series of events now known simply as 9/11, is a chilling case study. The nineteen men who hijacked the four airliners planned their heinous crimes deliberately and methodically. Years, decades, and generations of hatred for Israel and America fueled the fires of murder and destruction. The hatred of these terrorists ran so deep, they willingly gave up their own lives to destroy the lives of others.

But more than that, these murderers planned for years, obtaining pilot licenses, studying airline routes and schedules, carefully calculating the destruction of as many people as possible. Their hearts and minds spewing hatred and murder, they studied and planned for this evil act. (That night President George Bush would tell the American people in a televised address, "Today our nation saw evil, the very worst of human nature.")

WHY THE TERRORISM?

U.S. officials linked the terrorists to Osama bin Laden, a Saudi dissident and leader of the group Al-Qaeda. Bin Laden would be killed ten years later while hiding in Pakistan. But the hatred among the terrorists showed itself in a litany of destruction leading up to 9/11: the 1993 bombing of the World Trade Center in New York killing six and injuring one thousand; a car bombing in Saudi Arabia killing five U.S. military personnel; the 1996 bombing of a Saudi Arabia apartment building killing nineteen American military personnel and wounding four hundred people; the 1998 bombing of the U.S. embassies in Kenya and Tanzania, killing 224 and injuring thousands; the 2000 suicide bombing of the USS *Cole* in Yemen that killed seventeen sailors and injured thirty-nine.[1]

What is happening? Why does terrorism exist? What would motivate people to plan the murder and destruction of other people? Why does this evil exist?

WHY THE VIOLENCE UPON THE INNOCENTS?

Before we answer the question "Why does evil exist?" here are two more questions concerning violence in our world. *First, why are the innocent victims of violence?*

Lorraine Yaslowitz hugged and kissed her husband, Jeffrey, good-bye. Once outside, Jeffrey did something special for Calen, his five-year-old son. He turned on the emergency lights atop his police SUV so Loren and Calen could watch from inside. "Calen was all excited about that because he loves that," Lorraine recalled. "We were standing at the window, and we were waving at him and blowing kisses. . . . He just sat there and kept the lights on and then finally he took off," she said, her voice breaking up, "and that's going to be my baby's final remembrance of him."[2]

That very day in St. Petersburg, Florida, police officers Jeffrey Yaslowitz and Thomas Baitinger attempted to apprehend a criminal hiding in an attic. When they finally confronted the armed fugitive, both police officers were killed in the shootout.

Lorraine Yaslowitz described her husband: "If you were to have one word for him, it's 'devout.' He was devoted to what he was passionate about. He had a strong faith in Christ." But now officer Yaslowitz was dead as a result of a senseless killing by a criminal, leaving behind a young widow and three young children: Calen, age five, and two siblings, ages eight and twelve.[3]

Is God in control when senseless crimes occur, leaving broken hearts and destroyed families?

Some might say every police officer knows there is risk when in the line of duty. Yes, but there is also a God who could have saved them, perhaps by having the bullets graze them or striking a non-vital part of their bodies. Instead, Lorraine and her three children lost their father as he tried to uphold justice. Is God in control when senseless crimes occur, leaving broken hearts and destroyed families, including Christian families? Doesn't God watch over His people? Isn't that the promise of Scripture? How can we make any sense of this?

Second, why are the innocent unborn made victims of violence? From 1973–1994 unborn children in America lost their lives at the rate of 1.4 million per year through abortion.[4] Since the 1973 Supreme Court decision of Roe vs. Wade that legalized abortion, nearly fifty million of these procedures have been performed—an incomprehensible number of deaths of the innocent. Though abortion proponents argue that the issue is "a woman's right" to choose, the child within the womb has no rights and may forfeit his or her life at any time before birth.

WHAT IS HAPPENING IN NATURE?

When it comes to bad things happening to God's people, none is more perplexing than natural disaster. Floods . . . famines . . . earthquakes . . . Why are there so many disruptions in nature? Why does God permit such turbulence in nature that causes so much suffering and death?

In America, major flooding of rivers due to spring runoffs causes the loss of farmlands and sometimes livestock. During some summers, major hurricanes bring severe flooding and violent winds that destroy homes and claim lives in the Gulf states and along the Atlantic seaboard.

The opposite natural disaster, severe drought, destroys crops and creates famine. In Africa, insignificant rainfall during the first decade of the twenty-first century brought drought and famine. In 2000, the United Nations estimated that as many as 16 million people in seven countries were in danger. Three years of drought had destroyed crops and devastated the livestock in Ethiopia and six neighboring countries.[5]

> The 1984–1985 famine in Ethiopia claimed one million lives. In 2011, four million faced crisis in Somalia.

As I write this chapter, the worst drought in east Africa in sixty years has brought both malnutrition and death to several countries, most notably Somalia, where the rate of malnutrition among children is 58 percent. There "four million are in crisis . . . with 750,000 people at risk of death" by the end of 2011, according to the United Nation's food and security analysis unit.[6] Less than two decades earlier, the 1984–1985 famine in Ethiopia claimed one million lives.

Outside of death itself, one of the worst dangers posed by nature's havoc is homelessness. Without shelter, there is risk of chilling cold—or fierce heat. In 2010, a massive 7.0 magnitude earthquake struck Haiti with devastating effects. An estimated 200,000 people died, and an additional 250,000 were injured. But 1.5 million Haitians were left homeless. Although food supples were airlifted, many received little and remained exposed to the elements. The people of Haiti are still recovering today. How shall we understand this?

When a series of tornadoes rolled across Alabama's Tuscaloosa County in December 2000, many people lost their homes. Though most residents were spared (eleven died and 124 were injured),[7] they endured much hardship as they had to seek temporary shelter.

And some were not spared. I read of the twenty-six-year-old youth minister at Unity Baptist Church in Tuscaloosa found under the rubble with the rest of his family. James Crowder and his fifteen-month-old son, Wesley, were dead; the pastor's wife and two daughters survived, although with serious injuries. They were described as a model family.[8]

Why do these tragedies happen to God's people? Why is a young pastor's family broken through death? What is happening in nature? These are serious and difficult questions.

It's time to look for the answers. They are found in the Bible, God's Word to mankind. The answers do point to a God who cares. The Bible also points to a holy God who holds men and women accountable for their actions.

IN THE BEGINNING

When this world was first created, all was perfect. No violence, no hunger, no flooding. The Bible declares God's creation "was very good" (Gen. 1:31). Adam and Eve lived in unashamed bliss. Sickness, suffering, and death were not a part of their Edenic world.

Adam worked; he had a major task in observing the animals and correspondingly naming them (2:18–19). God also placed Adam "into the Garden of Eden to cultivate it and keep it" (2:15). What was involved? The Scriptures are not explicit, but Adam no doubt worked at planting and harvesting fruit and vegetable crops. Yet it was on an unspoiled earth, providing lavish, beautiful crops." But Adam never got tired; he never missed work because of the flu or fever.

Adam and Eve, his wife and helpmate, never got sick. They never quarreled; family abuse was unknown to them in their early marriage. Death was not a part of their experience. They lived in a perfect world, without trouble of any kind.

A FATAL DECISION

But then something happened. The tragedy is told in the third chapter of Genesis and it is key to understanding all suffering that has plagued humanity since that time. Adam and Eve chose to disobey God. As the head of the human race, Adam plunged all humanity into devastation and death through his one act of disobedience (Rom. 5:12).

Genesis 3:14–19, 22–24 explains the judgments of God upon man and woman. In raw form, the account explains the source of natural disasters—hurricanes, earthquakes, tornadoes—and, in fact, all human suffering. Sickness, family tragedies, and death all spring from people's sins against God and one another. Although Genesis 3 doesn't give us specific answers, it does help us understand why tragedies happen in this world. As one Christian counselor has stated, "We would all fare better in this world if we recognized that we live in a fallen world." That is a profound statement and an important factor in understanding why bad things happen to God's people.

What happened in Genesis 3? God placed man in the garden of Eden with a test to determine his obedience to God. If Adam obeyed God, he would lead the human race into eternal blessing; if he disobeyed God, he would sentence humanity to suffering and death. Satan, through the serpent (who must have been a beautiful creature before the fall), first tested Eve by offering her the fruit that God had forbidden (v. 1–5). And Adam, who was at her side and did not stop her (v. 6), agreed to partake as well.

THE MYSTERY OF EVIL'S SOURCE

But where did evil come from in the first place? Unfortunately, that is a mystery that will remain locked up in the counsel of the sovereign God. We know that God alone is eternal. Evil is not eternal. Evil first revealed itself when the angel Lucifer, more commonly known as Satan, rebelled against God (Is. 14:12–17; Ezek. 28:11–19). This was prior to the events of Genesis 3.

But there is no indication in Scripture concerning the origin of evil. It remains a mystery.

THE TEMPTATION

Satan raised doubt concerning God's command (Gen. 3:1). "Indeed, has God said?" he asked rhetorically. "Indeed, really?!" was the question of doubt he posed. He provoked Eve to question whether God had actually prohibited them from eating of a particular tree in the garden. He raised suspicion concerning the goodness of God—surely God would not withhold eating fruit from a particular tree! God would be dealing unfairly with His people. Eve responded to the doubt when she exaggerated God's prohibition by adding, "You shall not . . . touch it" (v. 3). God never said that, but people who doubt God's Word often will pervert it.

Envisioning success, Satan advanced his attack. He lied, saying "You surely will not die!" (v. 4). Satan laid the foundation of modern thought that denies the judgment of God with eternal consequences. Satan continued by telling a partial truth: "In the day you eat from [the fruit] your eyes will be opened, and you will be like God, knowing good and evil" (v. 5). Their eyes indeed would be opened, and they would definitely know good and evil, but Satan never enlarged on the consequences—suffering and death.

Had Adam and Eve obeyed God, they would have come to a knowledge of good and evil through obedience. They would know evil cognitively; now they came to know evil experientially—and the entire human race would be affected.

THE BEGINNING OF BAD THINGS

Satan's temptation was too much for Eve. He enticed her through the medium that is now common to all humanity: "the lust of the flesh, the lust of the eyes and the boastful pride of life (1 John 2:16). When Eve saw that "the tree was good for food [lust of the flesh], and that it was a delight to the eyes [lust of the eyes] and that the tree was desirable to make one wise [boastful pride of life]," she ate the fruit (Gen. 3:6). She also gave it to Adam and he too ate.

The effect of their eating was immediate. They now knew the difference between good and evil, but not in the way that they expected. They now knew about evil, but it was because of their own evil. Suddenly they sensed shame in their nakedness, and they sought to cover themselves (v. 7). Fellowship with God was disrupted. Instead of responding when they heard God's presence, they hid themselves (v. 8). They no longer sought His fellowship.

God called to Adam, giving him an opportunity to come and confess his sin, but Adam refused to acknowledge his guilt; he was more concerned about his nakedness than his disobedience to God's command (v. 10). When God quizzed him further, Adam initiated the first blame game. Instead of acknowledging his disobedience, he blamed Eve—and God Himself! He argued, "The woman whom *You* gave to be with me . . . " (v. 12, italics added). Adam implied God was at fault because He had given the woman to Adam.

He also blamed Eve: "*She* gave me from the tree, and I ate"

(v. 12). He suggests he would not have eaten the forbidden fruit if Eve had not given it to him. She was at fault, not he.

Eve likewise blamed another—she blamed the serpent (v. 13). The serpent was responsible. Interestingly, Eve acknowledged that she was deceived.

As a result of the sin of Adam and Eve, God pronounced a judgment on them, the serpent, and on the earth (vv. 14–19). What is described in these verses has affected all humanity from that day forward until the day that Jesus Christ returns to restore this fallen world and remove the curse and the judgment (Isa. 11:6–9; 65:17–25; Rev. 20:4). But until that time, all humanity will live with the effect of Adam's sin. There will be natural disasters, personal suffering—and death.

> As a result of the sin of Adam and Eve, God pronounced a judgment on them and on the earth.

THE WAR OF TWO WORLDS

The serpent was judged; he would feel the curse more than any other animal. By his very movement he would ingest the dust of the earth (Gen. 3:14). But God also directed His judgment toward Satan, the one acting through the serpent. Hostility and war would now confront Satan's seed (unbelievers and/or demons) and the seed of the woman (Christ and believers, but ultimately meaning Christ). But in a remarkable statement in Genesis 3:15, there is also the first announcement of the gospel. The seed of the woman—Christ—would bruise Satan's head: "He shall bruise you on the head, and you shall bruise him on the heel."

What is the meaning? A blow on the head is a death-inflicting blow. Through Christ's death on the cross Satan would be rendered powerless (Heb. 2:14). A war of two spiritual worlds began in the garden of Eden when man fell into sin. The effects of sin—suffering and death—remain in this present age. Yet Satan's power over believers is broken. God's people no longer need to live in fear of death and in subjection to Satan in this life. Despite living in a fallen world that still brings the ravages of disease and death, Satan's power through fear has been destroyed for God's people. It is the prerogative of God's people to live in triumph over tragedy; they can enjoy the peace of God in troubling circumstances. Many of God's saints have demonstrated this grace over the centuries.

SUFFERING IN CHILD BEARING

Because Eve was aligned with Adam in the first sin, she too experienced the judgment of God that would affect her descendants. Motherhood would be achieved only through pain and suffering. Pain becomes a new experience for Eve. In all her days on earth she had never experienced pain; she had no reference for it. In all her days until now Eve had enjoyed health, both physical and emotional. But all that would change. And all mothers throughout history would subsequently be subjected to pain (Gen. 3:16).

But the judgment was more than pain in childbearing. From now on women would experience pain of various kinds. Eve sought delight in eating the forbidden fruit; instead she and her descendants would experience pain and sorrow. And that is the history of mankind, pain and suffering. A cloud of misery has been cast over the human race through this initial sin.

SUFFERING IN THE NATURAL WORLD

Before sin entered the garden of Eden, the productivity of the land was lavish. The trees of the garden produced fruit in abdundance, without disease. Vegetable plants provided tasty food for Adam and Eve with minimal work on their part. No crop failures, no drought, no destruction from hostile insects.

But all that changed after Adam and Eve sinned. Like Eve,

Adam would also experience the consequences of his sin and disobedience. Instead of picking the fruit and vegetables in the garden with ease and delight, the produce would now come with great resistance. Enemy weeds would sprout and hinder the growth of the plants in the garden. God had judged the earth because of Adam's sin: "Cursed is the ground because of you; in toil you will eat of it all the days of your life. Both thorns and thistles it shall grow for you; and you shall eat the plants of the field; by the sweat of your face you will eat bread" (Gen. 3:17–19).

God had cursed the ground. Specifically, there were two major results. The soil would now no longer spontaneously provide the produce; it would only come by man's strenuous labor. Second, the produce would be meager; there would no longer be natural bumper crops.

OTHER EFFECTS OF THE FIRST SIN

The effects of Adam's sin are numerous. When I began ministry in the pastorate, I served a small country congregation. I well remember that first year of ministry in Manitoba. Because of the brief summers in western Canada, farmers frequently face a serious challenge in harvesting their crops before frost invades their fields. That summer was particularly cool and wet. When the fields would begin to dry, the rain would come again. The farmers were stymied at harvest time; they were unable to get their tractors and combines on the fields to harvest their crops. With the onslaught of the fall, one farmer determined to harvest his crop, wet or dry. As he drove his tractor onto the field, it immediately sank up to the axle in the quagmire. He was unable to accomplish his task. But rain turned to snow, and that winter the crops remained on the fields, covered with snow.

Those farmers could not harvest their crops. Unquestionably, the lost income from the missing crop sales created a financial hardship for many families. These were good people—they were

God's people—yet bad things happened to them.

Of course, this story could be multiplied thousands of times. Every year, farmers, ranchers, and others who depend on the products from the soil experience hardship. Frost, hail, drought, and flood all prevent farmers from properly enjoying the benefits of the soil.

In 1950 the Red River, which flows north and forms the natural boundary between the Dakotas and Minnesota, flooded. Communities on both sides of the Canadian-American border were inundated with the flood waters, which assumed the proportions of a gigantic lake. Fargo, Grand Forks, and even Winnipeg were flooded. My little hometown of Morris was also flooded, and the entire population was evacuated. I remember returning home with my widowed mother. From our front window I spotted a telephone pole that protruded from the water. Three feet of water covered the main floor of our house. Those hardwood floors were buckled, the furniture ruined. But the flood struck the preacher's home as well as the promiscuous person's house.

Why do these things happen? The answer is found back at the beginning of mankind. *All humanity*, including Christians, suffer as a result of the sin of our first parents. Their sin brought the fall of creation and the beginning of all natural disasters that have afflicted the earth since the beginning of time.

DEATH—THE ULTIMATE SUFFERING

So this is the underlying reason for all suffering. But that is not the end of the story. God told Adam he would labor strenuously to gain the produce of the ground "till you return to the ground, because from it you were taken; for you are dust, and to dust you shall return" (Gen. 3:19). This was yet the harshest judgment because of Adam's sin—the dust of death.

The expectation of death was foreign to Adam. Now death would invade the human race and spread its telling tentacles to all—rich and poor, educated and uneducated, young and old, godly and ungodly, sports heroes and spectators—all would now pass through death's door.

Humanly speaking, death is the ultimate bad thing that happens to all people, including God's people—who, of course, remain sinners, albeit redeemed sinners.

When we are young, little thought is given to death, but as we grow older, the prospect of dying becomes much more real. With age we come to understand our physical finiteness.

January 31, 2005, will forever remain etched in my mind and heart. My wife, Helen, accompanied me to the car that morning, carrying my mug of coffee as I was preparing to drive to the church where I would teach a theology course for Southeastern Baptist Seminary. As I backed off the yard, Helen stood at curbside, blowing me kisses. Then she stood at the curb waving at me until my car turned the corner at the end of the street. When I returned home that afternoon, I found the door locked—which was unusual since Helen always unlocked the door when she knew I was coming. I called, "Helen," but there was no answer. I walked around the corner into the kitchen and saw Helen lying on the floor. She was in heaven. Massive heart attack.

The grief and sadness I have experienced since Helen's homegoing have been enormous. I never got over the thrill of being married to Helen, but now I'm alone and no one can replace her. How do we cope with this? How can we understand this? Is God in control of events like this?

We experience death of our loved ones on an individual level, but death can be seen on a much wider scope. The devastation and death produced by the two great wars of the twentieth century engulfed much of the world. Tens of millions of people, military and civilian, died as a result of World War II. Six million Jews died in the Nazi Holocaust. A greater number of people—including believers in Jesus Christ—died at the hands of Joseph Stalin of the communist Soviet Union. Japan suffered the devastation of two atomic bombs.

In addition, many of God's people died in combat in Germany, in Korea, and in Vietnam. Added to that are the believers who have been criminally assaulted while leading a quiet life.

AMID SUFFERING, A PROMISE

As a result of Adam's sin, pain, suffering, and death have entered the realm of mankind, including God's people. Ultimately all tragedies in our world are traced to Adam's original sin recounted in Genesis 3.

But this is not the end of the story of human suffering and sorrow. While Genesis 3 explains the entrance of sin, it also promises a Savior. A caring God who loves us declares that a Redeemer will come. Suffering and death entered the human race in the garden, but in the fullness of the times Jesus Christ the Redeemer and Conqueror will return to write the final chapter that will resolve the suffering of God's people.

A DIVINE PURPOSE IN SUFFERING?

Still, questions surface. If sin, having penetrated the human race, is rampant, is mankind left to random acts of nature? Is the world, in its fallen estate, heading toward oblivion without any divine controlling hand? Since sin has entered the world, do bad things happen to God's people without any divine purpose?

In a world flawed by sin and selfishness, some may think mankind—including Christians—is left to blind fate and random acts of chaos. *Is God not in control? Is God sovereign?* How can all the tragedies of human suffering, especially that of Christians, be explained if God is in control?

These are important and very significant questions. In chapter 3 we begin to answer them.

3

Is God in Control?

I f mankind and the entire world stands in a fallen estate, are believers left to the random happenings of a fallen world or is God still sovereign and in control over the world?

Rabbi Harold S. Kushner, whose son suffered from a rapid aging disease called progeria and died at the age of fourteen, has grappled with the dilemma of suffering in this world. He and his wife—as any loving parents—suffered at the loss of their son. He found the traditional answers of God's sovereign control of all events completely unsatisfying. He does not believe there are reasons why things happen. Rabbi Kushner takes issue with the writer of Psalm 92 who wrote, "The righteous man will flourish like the palm tree" (Ps. 92:12). He concludes,

> The psalmist would have us believe that, given enough time, the righteous will catch up and surpass the wicked in attaining the good things of life. How does he explain the fact that God, who is presumably behind this arrangement, does not always give the righteous man time to catch up? Some good people die unfulfilled; others find

length of days to be more of a punishment than a privilege. The world, alas, is not so neat a place as the psalmist would have us believe.[1]

Is God in control of the tragedies of life that cause so much suffering and heartache? Where is God in those happenings? Rabbi Kushner concludes, "Can you accept the idea that some things happen for no reason, that there is randomness in the universe?"[2] In considering an earthquake or a hurricane hitting a populated area, or a drunken driver colliding his car with a green Chevrolet instead of a red Ford nearby, Kushner suggests,

> There is no reason for those particular people to be afflicted rather than others. These events do not reflect God's choices. They happen at random, and randomness is another name for chaos, in those corners of the universe where God's creative light has not yet penetrated. . . . it may be that God finished His work of creating eons ago, and left the rest to us. Residual chaos, chance and mischance, things happening for no reason, will continue to be with us . . . We will simply have to learn to live with it, sustained and comforted by the knowledge that the earthquake and the accident, like the murder and the robbery, are not the will of God, but represent that aspect of reality which stands independent of His will, and which angers and saddens God even as it angers and saddens us.[3]

IS GOD CAPABLE?

For Rabbi Kushner, God is not in control of this world. So in dealing with issues like illnesses, he concludes that God cannot heal; He will not act contrary to "nature." He states, "We can't pray that He make our lives free of problems; this won't happen and it is probably just as well. We can't ask Him to make us and those we love immune to disease, because He can't do that. . . . God does not want you to be sick or crippled." Then Kushner says God cannot control certain elements of this world, writing, "He didn't make you have this problem, and He doesn't want you to go on having it, but he can't make it go away. That is something which is too hard even for God."[4]

Kushner resolves the problem of human suffering by concluding that God would like to resolve the problem but cannot. Bad things happen because there is randomness—chaos in this world. And God is not in control. But that provides small comfort. Where is the comfort in acknowledging a God who is good but is too weak to control His creation?

THE SCRIPTURES SPEAK

Admittedly, comprehending the reason for human suffering is a giant philosophical dilemma. But we cannot arrive at a conclusion of resolving human suffering through philosophizing. Ultimately, we must arrive at our answers from Scripture—God's declaration and revelation to us—not from reason or experience, or how we interpret experience. We are incapable of understanding or interpreting all the bad things and tragedies that occur.

As we proceed to investigate the Scriptures, we will discover that God is indeed sovereign over the universe, over nations, over nature, and over individuals. How then shall we explain the bad things that happen? In some cases we will, in others we won't. If we could explain everything, we would have the mind of God. Of course, we don't. As almighty God declared through the prophet Isaiah, "'My thoughts are not your thoughts, nor are your ways My ways,' declares the Lord. 'For as the heavens are higher than the earth, so are My ways higher than your ways and My thoughts than your thoughts'" (Isa. 55:8–9).

We are too limited in knowledge, intelligence, and wisdom. Further, we don't see the entire picture. Sometimes, over the years, we can begin to see why certain bad things happened and see the value in them. At other times we will live, experience tragedies, and die without ever having resolved them in our minds.

As Paul completed writing three chapters dealing with the sovereignty of God, he exclaimed, "Oh, the depth of the riches both of the wisdom and knowledge of God! . . . For who has known the mind of the Lord, or who became His counselor? Or who has first given to Him that it might be paid back to him again?" The apostle concluded with a benediction of praise: "For from Him and through Him and to Him are all things. To Him be the glory forever. Amen" (Rom. 11:33–36).

> Paul exclaimed, "Who has known the mind of the Lord, or who became His counselor?"

Paul recognized both the sovereignty of God and the inability for mortals to fathom His sovereignty. That must also be our conclusion. Yet, as we will see, the sovereign God lets everything happen for a reason.

Is it significant to study the subject of God's sovereignty? Entirely. Years ago the great British preacher Graham Scroggie exclaimed, "He is at peace whose God is sovereign." A recognition of God's sovereignty will bring us peace that we cannot find elsewhere. How did my grandmother find peace? We never discussed it, but I'm certain it was her own simple trust that God knew what He was doing—without her understanding it.

A DAMAGED GAS PUMP

When Frank, a friend of mine, backed his car into a gas pump, he mused on the meaning of this in his life. He recognized that God is sovereign, and he was trying to understand how this fit into the picture. Of course, people have contemplated the meaning of many far more serious issues in life than backing a car into a gas pump. Does God deal with small things like backing into a gas pump? Or does He only intervene in major events? Or still, as deists hold, did He create the world and fling it into space to let it run on its own?

Perhaps the most significant question with which we must grapple is the sovereignty of God versus the goodness of God. Is God sovereign but not good so that bad things happen? Or is God good but not sovereign so that He is incapable of resolving certain things?

The resolution to these questions cannot come from our interpretation of life's events. We cannot begin to understand the significance of the whys and wherefores of life. But if we acknowledge that the Bible is the inspired and inerrant Word of God, then we have an authoritative source to investigate.

TEN DOLLARS FOR A CAR RIDE

One afternoon I was leaving the office for the lengthy drive home. As I was driving along a lonely stretch of road, the engine suddenly died and the steering froze. With great effort, I was able somehow to maneuver the car to the side of the road.

There, at the side of the road, I thought about the sovereignty of God. He could have had the car cease in a more convenient place. Then I remembered that a gas station was several miles up the road. I considered my options and realized they amounted to one good one: walk down the highway to the gas station. It was very windy and dusty, and rain was imminent.

As I began to walk, an elderly couple in a Cadillac stopped me to ask directions to the hospital. I explained where the hospital was; they thanked me and were about to drive away when I explained my dilemma to them.

"I'll give you ten dollars if you drive me to the gas station just up the road," I offered. The man looked at his wife, she shook her head, and they began to drive away. Suddenly the Cadillac stopped, and the man called me.

"Let's see the ten dollars," he demanded.

I gave him the money and climbed into the back of the Cadillac for the ride to the gas station.

How was the sovereignty of God reflected in this event? I can only guess. Ultimately, the motor in my car was ruined and we had to get a different car. Perhaps God recognized the car was unsafe and He used this to motivate me to buy a better car. Maybe there was a lesson on faith. Maybe He simply wanted me to contemplate His sovereignty in such a minor issue. Perhaps none of these reflect the real reason. Nonetheless, God is sovereign over *all* things.

GOD IS SOVEREIGN OVER ALL THINGS

A comprehensive statement of God's sovereignty is Ephesians 1:11: "[God] works all things after the counsel of His will." In this passage "all" is emphatic. In *all* things God is working. The verb "works" is a present participle, emphasizing that God is constantly at work, directing the affairs of the universe and the world—from nations and local governments, down to families, individual Christians, and non-believers. God is sovereignly working in *all* things. Without exception. God is at work in the "big" things and in the "small" things.

> Absolutely nothing happens outside the framework of God's eternal plan.

Can you mentally factor that? Do you recognize it? *The way we live, the peace we enjoy, will be determined by our genuine, sincere belief in the sovereignty of God.*

God works all things after the counsel of His sovereign will.

"His purpose" points to the sovereign decree of God. Nothing, absolutely nothing happens that is outside the framework of God's eternal plan and decree. This should bring only one response— peace.

"His will" further emphasizes His sovereignty. If God works all things according to His will, then there must be a divine plan for all things. If something (like "nature" or randomness) or some- one could prevent or frustrate the will of God, then that something or someone would have to be greater or stronger than God. But God alone is omnipotent. The eminent British biblical scholar F. F. Bruce concludes, "His will may be disobeyed, but his ulti- mate purpose cannot be frustrated, for he overrules the disobe- dience of his creatures in such a way that it subserves his purpose."[5]

AN ANTINOMY

Surely the ultimate bad thing that has occurred in the history of humanity is the death of Christ. Godless men rejected, beat, and killed Jesus Christ, the only One who ever lived a completely righ- teous life. Yet as the apostles assembled after having been threat- ened by the Sanhedrin, they exclaimed, "For truly in this city there were gathered together against Your holy servant Jesus, whom You anointed, both Herod and Pontius Pilate, along with the Gen- tiles and the peoples of Israel, to do whatever Your hand and Your purpose predestined to occur" (Acts 4:27–28).

The apostles recognized that Herod, Pontius Pilate, the Gen- tiles, and the Israelites were all responsible for the death of Christ, yet Herod, Pilate, and the others did what God had purposed and predestined to occur.

This may be an upsetting thought to some but it is a com- forting thought when the truth of Acts 4:28 penetrates our think- ing. We must understand, first of all, that this is an *antinomy*—a contradiction between two principles that are taken to be true. In this case, the two principles are an individual's ability to decide and

God's sovereignty.[6] Verses 27–28 teach that people are responsible for their actions but also that God is sovereign over all things that transpire.

Both elements are true: God is sovereign and people are responsible for their actions. When we eliminate one factor from the equation, error results. If we say that people are responsible for their actions but God has no part in it, then we eliminate God from His sovereignty. Conversely, if we say that God is sovereign over all things and hence people are not responsible for their actions, we eliminate a vital factor about which Scripture is entirely clear: People are indeed accountable for their decisions and actions.

> People are responsible for their actions but God is sovereign over all things that transpire.

Our finite minds cannot reconcile these two divergent truths—but both are nonetheless true. We simply recognize them, believe them, and do not try to reconcile them. We are limited in our human thinking.

THE WALL COMES DOWN

One evening in 1989, I sat in my living room, watching with fascination the news report from CNN televison. I called to my son and said, "Jeremy, come watch this with me. This is history in the making." And we sat together, watching the dismantling of the Berlin Wall. European communism in our time had died. It was hard to believe. My parents and grandparents, as well as my wife's, had suffered persecution and loss of their estates because of hostile, murdering communists. Now the era that had begun in 1917 was over.

How did it happen? Humanly speaking, numerous factors

can be suggested. Mikhael Gorbachev, premier of the Soviet Union, had volitionally made a decision to allow the dismantling of the Union of Soviet Socialist Republics, ruled by strong communists in Moscow for seven decades. Gorbachev had opened the Soviet Union to freedom.

Some credit American president Ronald Reagan as a major factor because he confronted the Soviet Union and put mounting pressure on them. On June 12, 1987, standing at the base of the Brandenburg Gate in West Germany near the Berlin Wall, President Reagan challenged Premier Gorbachev: "Mr. Gorbachev, open this gate! Mr. Gorbachev, tear down this wall!" And then, on November 8, 1989, the Berlin Wall opened. Six weeks later, on December 22, the Brandenburg Gate opened.

Yet behind all that happened in 1989, the sovereign *God* had determined that European communism would come to an end in 1989. And European communism ended in 1989.

GOD IS SOVEREIGN OVER THE NATIONS

God is sovereign over the nations. The prophet Isaiah, ministering in Israel from 760–700 B.C., looked ahead to the future day of Judah's captivity in Babylon and the nation's ultimate release from captivity. Isaiah named the ruler who would issue the decree to free Israel to return to Jerusalem and rebuild the temple and the city. Isaiah declared, "Thus says the Lord . . . 'It is I who says of Cyrus, "He is My Shepherd! And He will perform all my desire." And he declares of Jerusalem, "She will be built," and of the temple, "Your foundation will be laid"'" (Isa. 44:24, 28).

More than one hundred fifty years before the historical event occurred, Isaiah prophesied that God would raise up Cyrus, who would conquer nations. He would release the Israelites to return to Jerusalem and decree that Jerusalem would be rebuilt. In 539 B.C. Cyrus, ruler of the Medo-Persians, destroyed the great Babylonian empire and shortly thereafter issued a decree that was precisely in fulfillment of Isaiah's prophecy. God was controlling the nations of the world.

When Nebuchadnezzar, king of Babylon, had a dream, the Lord revealed the meaning of the dream to Daniel. The prophet exclaimed, "It is He who changes the times and the epochs; He removes kings and establishes kings" (Dan. 2:21). The Lord revealed the scope of Gentile history to Daniel. Of course, God could not know the scope of history *unless He had first determined the entire extent of Gentile history!*

Nebuchadnezzar's dream spotlighted an image that would represent the spectrum of Gentile history from the Babylonian empire (612–539 B.C.) until the end of the age when the Messiah will return to rule in righteousness over the earth (Dan. 2:36–45). The four kingdoms that God revealed to Daniel were Babylon, Medo-Persia, Greece, and Rome, including the final form of the revived Roman Empire at the end of the age. God sovereignly determined the Gentile nations that would rule over the course of human history. God also established that the Messiah would destroy those Gentile kingdoms and establish a righteous kingdom that would endure forever (vv. 44–45).

Later, Nebuchadnezzar declared of the Lord, "He does according to His will in the host of heaven and among the inhabitants of the earth; and no one can ward off His hand or say to Him, 'What have you done?'" (Dan. 4:35). God is sovereign over the angelic sphere in the heavens, and He is sovereign in the affairs of mankind on earth. God controls all events that transpire on earth; this is the clear teaching of Scripture.

World atlases and maps that are a few years old become outdated. Countries change. Borders and boundaries change. Countries divide. Yet behind all of the geographical changes is a sovereign God who is entirely in control of the nations. The Lord has "determined their appointed times and the boundaries of their habitation" (Acts 17:26). This means God marked out the boundaries of the nations, and assigned and fixed these boundaries—before creation![7] That is an amazing truth that's hard to grasp in our finite minds.

GOD IS SOVEREIGN OVER PEOPLE

Solomon, the great king of Israel, saw himself in relation to God: "The king's heart is like channels of water in the hand of the Lord; He turns it wherever He wishes" (Prov. 21:1). The heart reflects the volitional part of man—the place of his decision making. In this vivid illustration, Solomon recognized that the king's decisions were governed by the Lord just as channels that are dug in the earth determine where the water will flow.

Every fourth year, in November, American citizens go to the polls to elect the president of the United States. It is a free election, and citizens have the prerogative to vote Republican, Democratic, or independent. Yet when the ballots are ultimately counted, God has determined who will be the next president of the United States. "He removes kings and establishes kings. . . . He does according to His will" (Dan. 2:21; 4:35). For this reason, the apostle Paul admonished the Romans, "Every person is to be in subjection to the governing authorities. For there is no authority except from God, and those which exist are established by God" (Rom. 13:1).

GOD OVERRULES THE HEARTS OF PEOPLE

Prior to 1989, Paul Bubar, European director of Word of Life Fellowship, was flying to a European country. Sitting beside him was a Hungarian Jewish medical doctor. As they conversed, the medical doctor asked Paul about his business. Paul explained that he was involved in a ministry devoted to bringing the gospel to children and young people through camps and Bible clubs.

The doctor exclaimed, "That's what we need in Hungary! The communist leaders owe me one. You go and tell them I sent you and they need to provide an opportunity for you to have that kind of ministry in Hungary." Paul thought to himself, *Sure. I've heard that sort of thing before.*

Later, he decided to follow through on the doctor's offer. He arranged for a meeting with the Communist leaders in Hungary together with Harry Bollback, cofounder of Word of Life Fellowship. At their first meeting, the Communists offered a castle estate but demanded an exhorbitant rental fee. It was unacceptable, and Harry told them so. They decided to meet again. On the next occasion, the Communists told Harry they could use the castle and some eighty-five acres of land at Toalmas, about an hour east of Budapest. They explained their rental fee: Word of Life would have to agree to take some five hundred of their Hungarian youngsters each summer and train them in morality and ethics.

Harry Bollback could hardly believe his ears. Trying to repress his excitement, Harry told them he would sleep on it and tell them tomorrow. The next day Harry told them he would accept their offer. The Communists permitted Word of Life to come into Hungary and utilize the castle and campus at Toalmas for its ministry. And the rental fee was exactly that—Word of Life took hundreds of Hungarian youngsters and taught them the gospel of Jesus Christ!

Word of Life has maintained the ministry at Toalmas since that time, with hundreds of Hungarian youngsters trusting Jesus Christ as their personal Savior. In addition, young men and women are trained for ministry at the Bible institute on the castle property.[8]

How did it happen? Certainly communism is antithetical to the gospel. No Communist would deliberately invite Christians to bring the gospel to his country. Yet that is precisely what happened.

There is only one explanation—God is sovereign. Long ago Solomon wrote, "Many are the plans in a man's heart, but the counsel of the Lord, will stand" (Prov. 19:21). Communists may seek to oppose the gospel, but the Lord says communism will not prevail. God moves upon the hearts of the leaders so they make decisions that they would not normally make. God's sovereign decisions will prevail.

GOD CONTROLS THE EVIL OF PEOPLE

But what about all the sin in the world? God does not—perhaps cannot—control evil; is that not so? One thing is certain and foundational to this discussion: God is holy (Lev. 11:44); He has no relationship to evil (Ps. 5:4; 11:4–6). Yet if God is sovereign, then He is sovereign over all things—including evil, although He is never the author of evil.

The resolution lies in the antinomy (previously discussed) between the sovereignty of God and the responsibility of man. Man is responsible for his actions, but that does not frustrate the sovereign plan of God. His will and purpose will be accomplished. This is seen in Joseph's remark to his brothers: "And as for you, you meant evil against me, but God meant it for good in order to bring about this present result, to preserve many people alive" (Gen. 50:20). Joseph's brothers sinned against God and against Joseph in selling him into slavery in Egypt. God was never a participant in their sin, yet in God's sovereign plan He used their evil action to bring about good. God elevated Joseph in Egypt and rescued not only Jacob's family, but produced an entire nation of Israelites during their stay in Egypt.

But God's sovereignty over sin is ultimately seen in the death of Christ. In Acts 2:23 Peter indicts the people of Israel as he explains why Jesus died: "This Man, delivered up by the predetermined plan and foreknowledge of God, you nailed to a cross by the hands of godless men and put Him to death." Peter cites two reasons why Christ died. *The people were responsible.* He indicts the Israelites for killing Christ—they are guilty. And the Romans are also guilty because they actually nailed Christ to the cross, carrying out the horrible execution by crucifixion.

Yet Peter says *God had predetermined the death of Christ*. It was part of His sovereign "plan." God sovereignly superintends the affairs of this world. After His resurrection Jesus reminded the apostles "that the Christ would suffer and rise again from the dead the third day" (Luke 24:46). God's plan will be accomplished.

The point is important. Those who crucified Christ were guilty of a heinous crime. They were responsible. They acted out of a volitional decision of rejection and hatred against the Messiah. Yet God had predetermined the death of Christ according to His sovereign plan.

Today we understand God's wisdom, mercy, and grace in delivering up Jesus to crucifixion. It accomlished our redemption. We could never have achieved forgiveness, justification, and ultimately glorification without the atoning, sacrificial death of Jesus Christ. The infinite wisdom and purpose of God achieved this. Yet it occurred through the sinful acts of wicked men, and they are responsible for their criminal acts. But God, without any connection to their sin, brought good out of their evil acts. God is both good and sovereign.

TRYING TO GRASP THE INCOMPREHENSIBLE

This is an important lesson for us. Sometimes, years after a tragedy, we can see the good that has come out of a bad event. A man recently told me that his mother-in-law, who was a believer, had died. But, he volunteered, good came out of it. Her seventy-seven-year-old husband, who was an unbeliever, was saved several months after her death. This man could see the good that God was working, even though his mother-in-law had died.

But sometimes we will not see; sometimes we will never see or understand the reason for a tragedy. Could my grandmother ever fathom the divine reason why she buried nine of her ten children and was twice widowed? Probably not. Believers who watch their loved ones experience enormous pain in sickness, lingering for months of severe suffering before dying—can they understand God's purpose for the suffering? Probably not.

At such times we must rest in the assurance that God is all wise and all good. There is a sovereign plan behind all of the events of life, including the bad things, the tragedies that occur. The psalmist says, "The Lord is good; His lovingkindness is everlasting, and His faithfulness to all generations" (Ps. 100:5).

WHAT PROFESSOR HENDRICKS CONCLUDED

God is sovereign. In His sovereignty He may rescue us from our dilemma. Or He may choose to allow us to suffer, even to the point of death, and we may never in this life understand His sovereign plan or purpose. But God is still sovereign, wise, and good, and out of His sovereign plan good will come.

In January 1996, Howard Hendricks, distinguished professor at Dallas Theological Seminary, visited a doctor for removal of a small skin cancer.

Eight hours later, there was still more [cancerous cells] to remove. After more surgeries, with a large hole in his head and facing invasive surgery into his skull, Hendricks received warning of danger to his ears, eyes, and brain. Holding his wife's hand, he said, "Either God is sovereign or He is not. And, if He's not, we're in deep trouble. But I'm coming down on the side that He is."

After the operation, the doctor reported, "It's obvious God is at work in your life. This cancer went as far as it could go toward your ear without affecting your hearing, as far as it could go toward your eye without affecting your eyesight, and as far as it could go toward your brain without affecting your mind."

"If God had said to me, 'I'll give you another course,'"
quips Prof, "I would have said, 'Let's make it an elective.'"[9]

Our God is sovereign and He is good. The things that happen,
occur for good, whether He delivers us or not . . . and He has His
good reason, whether we understand it or not.

GOD IS SOVEREIGN IN THE ANGELIC SPHERE

Unfortunately, some people assign more authority to Satan
than he has. He is limited in his power and authority. The classic
example of Satan's parameters of authority is the Book of Job. The
opening chapter describes the angels coming before God to give
an account to Him with Satan among them (Job 1:6). A debate
ensues between the Lord and Satan, with Satan accusing Job of
acknowledging God only because of the material blessings he
receives from the Lord. When he challenges the Lord to allow
him to test Job, the Lord permits him, but with restrictions (Job
1:12; 2:6). An important conclusion can be drawn from this
encounter: *Satan cannot do anything to the child of God unless the
Lord allows it.*

We cannot conclude that Satan attacks believers for no purpose. Whenever it occurs (and who is able to determine what is
Satan-induced?), the Lord has allowed it and has put restrictions on Satan.

Further, God has given strong promises to believers concerning the Adversary. It is written, "The Lord is faithful, and He
will strengthen and protect you from the evil one" (2 Thess. 3:3;
cf., Ps. 121:7–8). Because the Lord is faithful, He will provide
strength for the believer so that Satan will not triumph over the
believer. First John 5:18 promises: "We know that no one who is
born of God sins; but He who was born of God keeps him and the
evil one does not touch him." Satan cannot ultimately overpower
believers; they are "safe in the arms of Jesus."

GOD IS SOVEREIGN OVER NATURE

Living in Florida, I have seen the devastation that hurricanes can wreak. In 1992 Hurricane Andrew destroyed hundreds of homes in south Florida, leaving a trail of destruction in its path. The category 5 hurricane had a wind speed of 196 mph just before landfall in Homestead, Florida. Days later it would move through the Gulf of Mexico and land in Louisiana. All told, Andrew caused $26.5 billion in property damage.[10] Surely there were Christians among those who lost their homes and all their belongings.

How can these people reconcile the sovereignty of God with this seemingly senseless destruction of property? Everything lost. Family treasures . . . furniture . . . keepsakes . . . pictures . . . Is God in control? Or is this "blind nature"—are these "random happenings"?

Yes, God is entirely sovereign over nature. Jesus said, "He causes His sun to rise on the evil and the good and He sends rain on the righteous and the unrighteous" (Matt. 5:45). The context emphasizes God's beneficence to believers and unbelievers alike. God controls the lightning (Job 38:25, 35) and thunder (1 Sam. 7:10); He sovereignly brings rain to cause the crops to grow (Job 38:26–28). God causes the snow to fall (Ps. 147:16) and brings the ice and freezes the rivers (Ps. 147:17); He speaks and the ice melts (Ps. 147:18). He brings wind (Ps. 147:18b), the hail, and the wind storms (Ps. 147:8). He causes the earthquakes (Job 9:6).

A final thought. When Jesus walked this earth He stilled the storm with a word (Matt. 8:26). He is still the same today (Heb. 13:8). He does not change nor does His power change. If He could intervene yesterday, He can intervene today.

LESSONS IN NATURE

Are there lessons to be learned from nature? Does God speak to mankind through nature? Indeed He does. Every earthquake, hurricane, tornado, and flood speaks of the judgment of God. It is

God's reality illustration, reminding an ungodly and unbelieving humanity that He is a righteous God—there is a day of judgment coming. When Helen and I lived in southern California, we saw the effects of an earthquake when the highway leading to Palm Springs was buckled like a piece of plastic. There is a message in these happenings. The sovereign God is speaking (cf. Rom. 1:18-20). These events in nature are harbingers of the ultimate judgment of God.

And what of the droughts and floods that occur in different places? Is there a divine message? Is God speaking to people? Certainly this was true in biblical times. God warned Israel that if the people would not obey His Word, He would withhold rain from their crops (Deut. 11:17; 28:24); conversely, if they obeyed Him, He would send rain and their crops would flourish (Deut. 28:12).

LESSONS LEARNED

When the Red River flooded parts of North Dakota, Minnesota, and Manitoba in 1950, there was enormous destruction. But were there lessons to be learned? Definitely. A church group came to town and distributed clothing—it was a great testimony to this church. Townspeople learned to work together. People became industrious. Contractors came to town, providing jobs for people. Young people volunteered and discovered the importance of work and of service. There was a new spirit in the community of working together and helping one another. By God's grace, the homes were repaired and life went on.

Perhaps we pay too little attention to the events in nature. Maybe we should ask ourselves some significant questions. Is God speaking to us and our nation through nature? Is He disciplining us? Is God withholding His blessing?

GOD'S GOODNESS IN NATURE

When Paul spoke to the pagan people at Lystra, he did not emphasize the Old Testament Scriptures as he did when he spoke to a Jewish audience. Paul appealed to nature. He reminded them of the goodness of God when "He did good and gave you rains from heaven and fruitful seasons, satisfying your hearts with food and gladness" (Acts 14:17). They were reaping the benefits of God's goodness when they harvested their crops. But God did it for a reason: "In the generations gone by He permitted all the nations to go their own ways; and yet He did not leave Himself without witness" (Acts 14:16–17). Although the nations were under judgment, God postponed judgment. God revealed Himself to them in nature, that they "should turn from these vain things to a living God" (Acts 14:15). That was the point of God's benevolence through nature. It should provoke people to see the goodness of God and turn to Him in faith and obedience. God controls the natural elements—and He speaks to mankind through the elements.

GOD'S WISDOM AND GOODNESS IN HIS SOVEREIGNTY

God's sovereign control and guidance provides comfort and peace to the believer. We are promised, "With Your counsel You will guide me, and afterward receive me to glory" (Ps. 73:24). The promise is explicit and comprehensive. God's sovereign guidance covers all of life. Through life and through the hallway of death, ushering us home into His presence—God's sovereign wisdom will guide us.

As Paul contemplated the sovereignty of God, he broke into a doxology of praise:

Oh, the depth of the riches both of the wisdom and knowledge of God! How unsearchable are His judgments and unfathomable are His ways! For who has known the mind of the Lord, or who became His counselor? Or who has first given to Him that it might be paid back to him again? For from Him and through Him and to Him are all things. To Him be the glory forever. Amen. (Rom. 11:33–36)

On September 15, 1999, Larry Gene Ashbrook invaded Wedgwood Baptist Church in Fort Worth, gun in hand. When his shooting spree was over, eight people had lost their lives, including Ashbrook. Many families suffered physically, and the entire church suffered the emotional trauma of the tragedy.

Many were trying to sort out the relationship of God to this tragedy. Jeff Laster, a student at Southwestern Baptist Theological Seminary at the time of the shooting, "said the tragedy strengthened his belief in God's sovereignty and protection. . . . When Ashbrook entered the foyer, a cigarette dangling from his lips, Mr. Laster stood to greet him. Ashbrook pulled out a pistol and fired a shot that tore into Mr. Laster's left abdomen and through five internal organs before lodging in the right side of his back." Next he killed Sydney Browning "with a shot to the head." Laster later heard others at the church who weren't shot later say they were thankful that God protected them. He later told a reporter,

> What does that say in my case? I got shot. . . . What does that say about Sydney and Shawn Brown and other people who were killed? If God protected [those who weren't shot], what did he do for us? I wondered about that. I don't think that God slipped up and wasn't quick enough to catch the bullet or something. . . . Because I trust in Him doesn't mean I am not going to be shot or not going to have cancer or not be in a car wreck. His protection came in the cross. . . . If I had died the same night that Sydney did, my protection is that I have eternal life afterward.[11]

Dan Crawford, coauthor of *Night of Tragedy, Dawning of Light,* a book about the shooting and its consequences, said that the death of Kristi Beckel during the church shooting may have helped sustain the lives of as many as seventy people. Survivors of the shooting have appeared on television and radio and have spoken at both Christian and secular functions. A reporter for *World* magazine wrote one year after the deadly shooting, "Some view those media appearances, during which Wedgwood survivors often shared the gospel message, as evidence of God's turning evil into good. 'God uses the broken things, the humblest things for His glory,' [survivor] Mr. Meredith told his congregation."[12]

GOD'S SOVEREIGNTY IN OUR SUFFERINGS

God is sovereign. In His sovereignty He may rescue us from our dilemma. Or He may choose to allow us to suffer, even to the point of death, and we may never understand His sovereign plan or purpose. But God is still sovereign, wise, and good, and out of His sovereign plan good will come.

Nothing is outside the sphere of God's sovereign rule. Absolutely nothing. It is our prerogative to rest in the assurance of God's sovereign goodness, or we can can fret over the tragedies of life and become bitter. We are called to walk by faith, not sight, trusting the wisdom and goodness of God in the darkness.

4

---•---

Is God Sovereign over Evil?

The evils of World War II, with its many cruelties and atrocities, particularly against the Jewish people, have been well documented. Adolf Hitler was determined to exterminate the Jewish people—and the Holocaust became one of the pillars of the Nazi agenda.

Under Hitler and the Nazi military that bore the national socialist flag into war, nazism conquered much of Europe. In 1940, the Nazis invaded the Netherlands with their evil agenda. But God was at work in protecting His chosen people. Some Dutch Christians came to the aid of Jewish people. For example, the ten Boom family became active in the underground resistance movement; thirty members of the ten Boom family committed themselves to hiding and rescuing Jewish people. They built a secret room in Corrie ten Boom's bedroom. It was about thirty inches deep but able to hide six people. When the Nazis invaded their home in 1944, six people were in the ten Boom hiding place.

But on February 28, 1944, the Gestapo, the secret German

police, raided the ten Boom home and arrested all thirty members of the extended family, including Corrie, her brother, her two sisters, and her father. They were sent to the Scheveningen prison; there Corrie's father died some ten days later. The cruel concentration camps awaited. Corrie and her sister Betsie were first sent to the Vught concentration camp and then to Ravensbruck, where Corrie's sister Betsie died on December 16, 1944. In her final moments before death, Betsie told Corrie, "There is no pit so deep that He is not deeper still."[1]

The question asked of every war, of every injustice, is "Where is God?

In late December 1944, prison officials released Corrie ten Boom. She returned to the Netherlands where she was reunited with her remaining relatives. But now, how would they deal with the emotional trauma of family members and many, many others who had been ruthlessly killed? Corrie sought reconciliation as the solution. When she was in Munich, after having spoken on forgiveness, she saw a heavy man in a gray coat standing with others. Corrie suddenly envisioned the man in a uniform: he had been an SS guard in a concentration camp.

The man approached Corrie and told her he had been a guard at Ravensbruck. But he had now accepted Christ as his Savior and was seeking forgiveness: "I have become a Christian. I know that God has forgiven me for the cruel things I did there, but I would like to hear it from your lips as well. *Fraulein* . . . will you forgive me?" and he thrust his hand toward Corrie.

Corrie's sister had died at Ravensbruck—could Corrie forgive him? *Jesus help me!* Corrie prayed silently. *I can lift my hand; I can do that much. You supply the feeling.* With that, she thrust her hand toward the man's outstretched hand. Tears raced down Corrie's face as she exclaimed, "I forgive you, brother! With all my heart."[2]

The question asked of every war, of every injustice, is "Where is God? Is He in control?" In something so destructive as war, bringing hardship to every family—and death to some—many wonder whether God is really sovereign in an evil world.

Corrie and her sister Betsie concluded God is sovereign and watched over them despite their imprisonment, physical suffering, and in the case of Betsie, death. They recognized He has control over all things, including the tragedies of life. Years later, Corrie would travel, telling others about her good God, of how she could forgive a prison guard, and of how God cares for every person. Many have read Corrie's story in *The Hiding Place* and its sequel, *Tramp for the Lord*. Untold numbers of people have come to Jesus Christ or been revived to serve Him, or have learned to forgive others because of the testimony of Corrie ten Boom.

Yes, God is sovereign over the difficult events in life—and He has a purpose in these events. Sometimes we can understand the events—sometimes we will not understand them. But we trust in the sovereign, loving God.

BAD THINGS HAPPEN TO A GODLY YOUNG MAN

There are biblical examples of bad things happening to believers. But those bad things result in great good when funnelled through the design of a sovereign, good, and wise God.

One of these examples is Joseph. There is no record of sin in Joseph's life. He is seen as a God-fearing man who sought to please and obey God to his own detriment and suffering. And Joseph suffered considerably.

Joseph experienced the animosity of his brothers while he was only a teenager. While pasturing sheep with his brothers, he told his father about his brothers' sinful practices, immediately incurring the hatred of his brothers (Gen. 37:2). Jacob's favoritism toward "the son of his old age" intensified their bitterness (vv. 3–4). The father's gift of a beautiful, colorful tunic to Joseph verified the father's favoritism and cemented their hatred for Joseph. That hatred and envy would culminate in numerous bad things happening to Joseph.

The brothers' hatred for Joseph climaxed when Joseph told them of his dream. He dreamed that he and his brothers were binding sheaves in a field, and while his sheaf stood upright, the other sheaves bowed down to his sheaf. Clearly, Joseph's dream implied that his brothers would bow down to him, giving Joseph homage (v. 7), a highly repugnant thought to his brothers. In a subsequent dream Joseph saw the sun, moon, and eleven stars bowing down to him, suggesting that his parents and brothers would one day bow down to him. That was unthinkable! Because of this, Joseph's brothers despised him and hated him more than ever.

Their hatred for this righteous young teenager was so intense, some wanted to kill him. But in listening to Reuben, the oldest brother, they instead threw Joseph into a pit and eventually sold him to Midian traders who were on their way to Egypt (vv. 21–22, 28). Once they were in Egypt, the Midianites sold Joseph to Potiphar, Pharaoh's officer and captain of the bodyguard (v. 36).

IS THERE PURPOSE IN THE TRAGEDIES OF LIFE?

Bad things were happening to this righteous teenager. His father's favoritism and his own candor had brought the envy and resentment of his brothers and now slavery in Egypt. But God had not abandoned him. It was no "accident" that Joseph was taken to Egypt; it was not merely "circumstantial" that the Midianites sold Joseph to Pharaoh's officer. God was at work in all the events that were happening to Joseph so that good would ultimately come from the bad.

It is important when difficulties come our way and we cannot understand them, that we recognize that God in His sovereignty is directing the affairs to bring good out of the bad. Though often we will not understand the events, we can trust our sovereign God who rules over all and controls all things.

While he was in Egypt, God protected and cared for Joseph. Several times the Scripture emphasizes: "The Lord was with Joseph" (Gen. 39:2, 21). What does it mean that the Lord was with Joseph? Even though Joseph was sold to Potiphar, because the Lord was with Joseph, "he became a successful man" (v. 2). The Lord's blessing on Joseph was so evident, even Potiphar noticed "how the Lord caused all that [Joseph] did to prosper in his hand" (v. 3). As a result, Joseph was promoted to prominence in Potiphar's court, serving as superintendent. When Potiphar noticed that his household was being blessed because of Joseph's service, he entrusted everything into Joseph's care. God was watching over his child in a foreign country.

MORE TROUBLE FOR A GODLY YOUNG MAN

But Joseph's success and his handsome appearance set up another confrontation with evil. Potiphar's wife began making overtures to Joseph, enticing him to sleep with her. Joseph saw the sin for what it was, an affront to God; ultimately it was sin against God (v. 9). But Potiphar's wife persisted in her advances, and one day, when the servants were absent, she caught Joseph by his coat and demanded, "Lie with me!" (v. 12). Joseph had made his decision long before. He left the coat in her hand and fled. When she saw that she had been repulsed, she turned against Joseph and accused him of attempting to molest her. In his anger Potiphar had Joseph imprisoned.

> Remember that the trial, the difficulty, is not the end of the story.

Hadn't Joseph been morally upright? Hadn't he been faithful

to the Lord and obeyed His laws? Why were these things happening to him? Why was he in prison? Many of God's people ask similar questions. Amid our trials we must also remember that the trial, the difficulty, is not the end of the story. Joseph was in prison, but that was not the end of the story. He would not remain in prison.

Even though Joseph was imprisoned, God had not abandoned His child. He never does. His abiding presence is certain. He has promised, "I will never desert you, nor will I ever forsake you" (Heb. 13:5). That is a promise of God that is always true. We may experience a difficult ordeal, feeling alone and abandoned, but God never will abandon us. It is imperative that we remember God's faithfulness and His continuing, loving presence with us in our difficult circumstances.

GOD'S KINDNESS TO A PRISONER

Even in prison God's kindness to Joseph was evident. The prison warden put Joseph in charge of all the other prisoners; he didn't even supervise Joseph "because the Lord was with him; and whatever he did, the Lord made to prosper" (Gen. 39:23). Surely a believer's false imprisonment could result in the depth of discouragement. Yet here, in prison in a foreign country, God was with Joseph and gave him success in everything he did.

Undoubtedly, we come into situations we do not enjoy, we look at the circumstances, and we despair. We fail to see the sovereign hand of God. We fail to see the divinely ordained circumstances controlling the events whereby good will ultimately come from evil. Evil will not triumph. Good will triumph under the sovereign majesty of Jesus Christ.

When the king's cupbearer and baker were also imprisoned, Joseph interpreted their dreams. The cupbearer promised to speak to Pharaoh about Joseph when he was released, but he failed to do so. Instead, Joseph was forgotten and remained in prison for two years. How long would those two years have felt for Joseph? When we are in unpleasant circumstances the time seems endless. We feel as though we have been in the difficulty forever and that it will never go away. Joseph had lived righteously before the Lord, yet he was in prison for two years and the man who had the ability to speak on his behalf had forgotten him.

When Pharaoh had a dream that no one could interpret, the cupbearer finally remembered Joseph. God sovereignly had Pharaoh dream those dreams so the man who had been in prison would remember Joseph. Pharaoh was alerted and Joseph was summoned into his court to interpret his dreams of an eventual famine.

GOD'S PROMINENCE IN THE YOUNG MAN'S LIFE

We have seen God's sovereign care for Joseph—and for all of His children—in suffering. Now, however, the Scripture reveals that Joseph was also fully conscious of God's goodness to Him. When Joseph was summoned to interpret Pharaoh's dreams, he reminded Pharaoh that he could not do it. "*God* will give Pharaoh a favorable answer" was the young man's reply (Gen. 41:16, all italics added). Joseph's recognition of God's presence continued: "*God* has told to Pharaoh what He is about to do . . . *God* has shown to Pharaoh what He is about to do . . . the matter is determined by *God*, and *God* will quickly bring it about" (vv. 25, 28, 32).

GOD'S SOVEREIGN DESIGN BECOMES EVIDENT

What a lesson! Instead of groveling in self-pity over our difficulties, we should remember God's controlling care for us. He has not abandoned us any more than He didn't abandon Joseph.

Because God gave Joseph the interpretation of Pharaoh's dreams, Joseph rose to prominence in Pharaoh's court. Pharaoh appointed Joseph prime minister over Egypt. In his position of authority Joseph prepared for the coming seven years of famine by having the people store food. But the coming famine would also affect God's people—Joseph's family in Canaan. When Jacob realized there was grain in Egypt, he sent his ten sons to Egypt to buy food. It was God's purpose in bringing Jacob and his family to Egypt: (1) so they might have food; (2) so they would escape the pollution of the pagan Egyptians; (3) so they would become a great nation. When the Israelites left Egypt 430 years later, they came out as a nation of 2.5 million people.

But what was the process by which God accomplished His purpose with Joseph and his family? It began when Joseph interpreted his dreams to his brothers. That resulted in his brothers' hatred for Joseph . . . that resulted in them selling Joseph into slavery in Egypt . . . that resulted in Joseph working for Potiphar . . . that resulted in Joseph being tempted by Potiphar's wife . . . that resulted in Joseph being thrown into prison . . . that resulted in Joseph interpreting the cupbearer's and baker's dreams . . . that resulted in Joseph interpreting Pharaoh's dreams . . . that resulted in Joseph's release from prison and rise in prominence in Pharaoh's court . . . that resulted in Egypt preparing for the coming famine . . . that resulted in Jacob's family coming to Egypt. Is there evidence of the controlling, sovereign hand of God in these events? Indeed.

When we encounter bad things in our lives—illness, loss of a job, financial reversals, tragedies in the home—we focus on the singular event. And we fail to see God's sovereign design at work, bringing good out of bad. We look at the immediate; God sees and plans the future. We cannot imagine how good can come out of bad; yet, given enough time—and perspective—the good triumphs over the bad.

BAD THINGS CAN HAVE A GOOD RESULT

When the aged Jacob died, the brothers became alarmed, thinking Joseph would seek vengeance against them now that their father was dead. But Joseph responded in the classic statement: "As for you, you meant evil against me, but God meant it for good in order to bring about this present result, to preserve many people alive" (50:20). Joseph's brothers had evil designs on him; they hated him and determined to kill him. Only by the intervention of Reuben was his life spared, but the brothers still sold Joseph into slavery in Egypt. The teenager was removed from his family and his country to a foreign land to serve as a slave.

Yet what was meant as evil against Joseph—and what would have been difficult for him to understand for many years—would turn into good through the design of a sovereign, loving God. The brothers had sought to kill Joseph. Yet through their evil deed, God brought about good, not for only one person, but for an entire family that would grow into a great nation! Who can fathom the mystery of the wisdom of God? Surely Paul's outburst of praise should be ours as well:

> Oh, the depth of the riches both of the wisdom and knowledge of God! How unsearchable are His judgments and unfathomable His ways! For who has known the mind of the Lord, or who became His counselor? Or who has first given to Him that it might be paid back to him again? For from Him and through Him and to Him are all things. To Him be the glory forever. Amen. (Rom. 11:33–36)

We try to interpret the events that happen to us while we are in them, but it is impossible. It may be years before we gain insight into why certain things happened to us. Or we may never know in this life. Yet if God is sovereign (and He is) and if He is loving, good, and kind (and He is), then the events that happen to us are not simply nature gone awry. Nor is evil gaining the upper hand. God is in control of *everything* that happens, and He will bring it to a good conclusion, whether in this life or in the life to come, and whether we understand it now or not.

GOD CAUSES ALL THINGS TO WORK TOGETHER

The classic passage that many believers turn to is Romans 8:28: "And we know that God causes all things to work together for good to those who love God, to those who are called according to His purpose." This is a beautiful and important truth reminding us of God's sovereignty in using everything in our lives for our good. Since God is sovereign and good, then the circumstances that transpire in our lives have been sifted through His sovereign, wise, and loving hands. And they function for our spiritual good.

The context of this great passage is important for our understanding. When we experience difficulties and suffering in life, we become confused and do not know how to pray. But the Holy Spirit helps us in our weaknesses. At that point of our confusion the Holy Spirit intercedes for us by praying for us (see v. 26.) He prays on our behalf—but how? Yet a prior question must be: do we pray correctly? Do we fully understand our circumstances to pray that the difficulties and problems we experience will be resolved in the right way? No, we don't. But if the Holy Spirit, the third person of the Triune God, prays for us, He will always pray correctly.

What is the inference? It means that when the Holy Spirit intercedes for us, He takes our prayers, corrects them, and carries them to the Father. Alan Johnson wisely states, "Our problem is not ignorance of the *form* of prayer (how), but our weakness is an inability to articulate the *content* (what), that is, what we should ask for especially in sufferings that will meet our needs and at the same time fulfill God's will."[3]

Since the Father knows our hearts, even though we cannot express our needs properly, He responds to the corrected, intercessory prayer of the Holy Spirit (vv. 26–28). And since the Holy Spirit and the Father are both one in the Godhead, the Holy Spirit prays in unity with the Father's will, and the Father readily answers the prayer of the Holy Spirit because it is in harmony with the divine will. As a result, "God causes all things to work together for good to those who love God, to those who are called according to His purpose."

Again, we must understand this vital verse in its context. Unquestionably, there are times when we have agonized, prayed, and pleaded with God. Yet the resolution is so different from what we expect. But biblically, all things are working together for good. Our problem is that we do not have God's perspective. God sees our lives with His perfection, His infinite wisdom, and magnanimous love. We are narrow in our vision. We think the resolution to the bad things that happen to us *must* be resolved in a certain way. That difficult supervisor at my job, surely the only resolution to him harrassing me is for him to be removed. The unbelieving spouse who has not responded to the believer's witness, certainly God would sanction a divorce in this case. The illness that plagues me, why doesn't God answer my prayer and heal me? But the Lord says, "My thoughts are not your thoughts, nor are your ways My ways" (Isa. 55:8).

> God views "good" as spiritually good. God's ultimate purpose is always to mature us spiritually.

There is another aspect of Romans 8:28 that needs to be considered. It says, "God causes all things to work together for good." In context, "all things" refers to suffering (cf. v. 18). These sufferings include a wide variety of things that happen to us—illnesses, hardships, problems, adversities. But what is our understanding of "good"? Likely, we perceive "good" as being financial solvency, good health, and good relations at home and at work. We tend to view "good" as physically and materially good. But how does God view "good"? Unquestionably, God views "good" as spiritually good. God's ultimate purpose for us is always to mature us spiritually.

Whatever God designs to happen to us is for our spiritual

good. We may not see the value of our illnesses, sufferings, and trials. But it is through those difficulties that we listen to the voice of God and allow Him to develop us spiritually.

What a difference this will make if we learn to look at the events that impact our lives as being God's trumpet call to a higher spiritual plane.

PAUL'S PREDICAMENT—OR OPPORTUNITY?

The apostle Paul's life is interesting to study. He was one who was falsely accused, yet God used Paul's suffering for the extension of the kingdom of God. Wherever Paul went, his steps were dogged by the unbelieving Jews who sought to silence him. In Caesarea, after the Jews had again accused him of treason, heresy, and temple desecration, Paul appealed to Caesar (Acts 25:11). As a Roman citizen, this was Paul's privilege. Because of his appeal, Paul was taken to Rome where he remained under house arrest for two full years (Acts 28:30).

During this time the apostle was constantly chained to a Roman soldier. He was eventually declared innocent and released, but I wonder how I would feel, being falsely accused and imprisoned—and chained for twenty-four hours a day for two years? Could I see the hand of God in it?

Paul did. For one thing, he realized he could receive numerous guests, including unbelievers and critics with whom he readily shared the gospel. During his two-year imprisonment Paul constantly proclaimed the gospel—unhindered (28:23, 31)! Some of those who heard Paul were converted to faith in Christ (v. 24).

Paul didn't look at his chains; he looked at the sovereign hand of God in his imprisonment. He saw it as a divine opportunity. It "turned out for the greater progress of the gospel" (Phil. 1:12). Paul blazed a trail for the gospel into the royal court of Rome! The whole praetorian guard, Tiberius's special hand-picked soldiers, heard the gospel because of Paul's imprisonment.

Paul may have been constantly chained to a guard, but he had a captive audience! The guards couldn't get away from him! Each guard, one by one, heard his majestic prayers, his conversations with other Christians, his explanation of the gospel to the Jews. They heard him dictate letters. The result was that some of the Roman soldiers believed and carried the gospel further into the courts of imperial Rome. Paul saw the sovereign hand of God in his imprisonment.

> Each guard, one by one, heard his majestic prayers, his explanation of the gospel to the Jews.

LETTERS FROM PRISON

Paul's imprisonment also produced the beloved letters to the Ephesians, Philippians, Colossians, and to Philemon. What Christian cannot testify that these divinely inspired words of God through the apostle have encouraged, instructed, and blessed the believer? But these lovely letters came through suffering. The apostle Paul endured two years of chained imprisonment so that over two millennia countless millions of believers would be spiritually refreshed through the letters he wrote in prison.

Consider the following verses, written by the apostle while in prison:

- Blessed be the God and Father of our Lord Jesus Christ, who has blessed us with every spiritual blessing in the heavenly places in Christ. (Eph. 1:3)
- In Him we have redemption through His blood, the forgiveness of our trespasses, according to the riches of His grace. (Eph. 1:7)

- By grace you have been saved through faith; and that not of yourselves, it is the gift of God; not as a result of works, that no one may boast. (Eph. 2:8–9)
- Be strong in the Lord and in the strength of His might. Put on the full armor of God. (Eph. 6:10–11)
- For to me, to live is Christ and to die is gain. (Phil. 1:21)
- . . . having the desire to depart and be with Christ (Phil. 1:23).
- Rejoice in the Lord always. (Phil. 4:4)
- Be anxious for nothing, but in everything by prayer and supplication with thanksgiving let your requests be made known to God. And the peace of God, which surpasses all comprehension, shall guard your hearts and your minds in Christ Jesus. (Phil. 4:6–7)
- Strengthened with all power, according to His glorious might, for the attaining of all steadfastness and patience; joyously giving thanks to the Father. (Col. 1:11–12)
- Christ in you, the hope of glory. (Col. 1:27b)
- Set your mind on the things above, not on the things that are on earth. For you have died and your life is hidden with Christ in God. (Col. 3:2–3)

All these beautiful verses came from prison . . . amid suffering. God took the harsh experience of Paul's imprisonment in Rome and fashioned good out of them. The benefits of Paul's suffering still provide comfort, encouragement, and blessing to God's people around the world—two millenia after they were written.

THE EVIL OF A ROMANIAN DICTATOR

The revolution in 1989 that toppled Romania's Communist hardline dictator Nicolae Ceausescu was sparked by a Protestant pastor, Laszlo Toekes. During the days of communist power, Toekes resisted Communist oppression by campaigning for religious and ethnic rights. The Communists suspended him from ministering to his congregation. But he refused to comply with the order, stating, "I am among those who have had enough of silence and being silenced."

He was harrassed; masked men broke into his house at night and threatened to kill him and his pregnant wife. Later, he was abducted and severely beaten by security guards. Toekes finally took refuge in his church, and hundreds of people formed a human chain around it, preventing his arrest. This resulted in the massacre of tens of thousands of people in Timisoara, but it triggered the revolution, and freedom ultimately prevailed.[4]

One Christian allowed bad things to happen to him so that good might ultimately prevail. Pastor Laszlo Toekes suffered physically, but the rich reward is evident to this very day. Romania is a free country today. The gospel is widely proclaimed; churches are growing and evangelizing their communities. Bible colleges are teeming with students preparing for the gospel ministry. All this because one man suffered physically but trusted God to bring good out of bad. Can we begin to see that God will bring good out of the bad in our circumstances?

THE POWER OF ENDURING EVIL AND SUFFERING IN ROME

Paul's imprisonment encouraged his friends to proclaim the gospel with even greater boldness (Phil. 1:14). It became well known that Paul's arrest occurred because he was a Christian. This simply inspired other believers to greater courage in bold proclamation of the gospel (Phil. 1:13). Surely, God's ways are mysterious. The gospel received free advertising! Christianity was discussed, and Paul's fellow believers took advantage of the current interest in Paul and Christianity by preaching the gospel. When Paul heard of it, he was filled with joy because the message of Christ was being proclaimed (Phil. 1:18).

THE POWER OF ENDURING EVIL AND SUFFERING IN CHINA

Has communist oppression of Christians in China silenced the church? Did Watchman Nee's imprisonment curtail evangelism in China? No. The suffering of God's saints encourages others to proclaim His Word more vigorously than ever before. The church of Jesus Christ is alive and well in China, flourishing though it continues to be persecuted. The suffering of some believers encourages others to grasp the baton and press toward the mark of the upward call of God. Even though bad things happen to God's people, greater good is the result.

In April 2011, in Beijing, China, the communist officials pressured the owners of a building to evict the 1,000 members of Shouwant Church, which was leasing the building for worship. It created a dilemma for the believers. If they chose to worship outdoors, members of the unregistered church could suffer reprisal from the communist government. Yet, the courageous church leaders explained in a letter to the congregation: "Sunday worship is the most basic necessity for Christians in their life of faith."[5]

On April 10, 2011, the "police blocked the designated meeting area and detained more than 160 Christians armed with Bibles and hymn sheets. . . . at least two church leaders remained under house arrest, and many church members said police were monitoring their movements." The next Sunday nearly fifty members who attempted to worship outdoors were detained with all of the church leaders remaining under house arrest. "Some church members had suddenly lost jobs and faced eviction from their homes."[6]

But the courageous Chinese church leaders encouraged others. The pastors said, "As the church of Jesus Christ, we should not change our mode of Sunday worship just because someone or some entity decides that we may or may not use a particular meeting place." The church leaders encouraged their people: "Do not resist, let them take us away, just like a lamb to the slaughter. In our hearts, we know we gather for worship—and for the sake of worship, we will pay the price."[7]

Perhaps this is what Paul thought of when he exclaimed, "For to you it has been granted for Christ's sake, not only to believe in Him, but also to suffer for His sake" (Phil. 1:29). Believing and suffering go together in the life of a believer. Bible commentator Gerald Hawthorne says the believers at Philippi "are suffering because they are on Christ's side. They have believed the gospel of Christ (v. 27a). They have set themselves to preserve and propagate this gospel (v. 27b). They have taken their stand with Christ. As a consequence they have put themselves on a collision course with hostile forces abroad in their world that are opposed to Christ. It is inevitable then that they suffer."[8]

> God extends grace—supernaturally—to the believer in the time of suffering.

Even as Christ suffered because He was righteous, so believers, identified with Christ in His righteousness, will also suffer. "Thus, as the saints suffer for righteousness's sake, they substitute for their absent Lord not only in the task of preaching the message He has given them but also in suffering for His sake and in His stead."[9]

"Suffer" is emphatic in the biblical passage (Phil. 1:29). But how can a believer endure the suffering? The phrase "It has been granted" comes from the root word *charis,* meaning "grace." It emphasizes that God extends grace—supernaturally—to the believer in the time of suffering. The Lord enables believers to supernaturally bear suffering at such a time.

When evil or injustice leads to suffering, let's remember that God remains sovereign. Sometimes we recognize it amid the pain; at other times our children, grandchildren, and friends will recognize the spiritual value of the suffering. Know that God never changes. He is the all-powerful, all-wise, and all-good God. There is a reason for our suffering and we must rest in that truth. He works all things for our good.

TRUST GOD, NOT SELF

Paul wrote to the Corinthians, telling them of his sufferings in Asia (2 Cor. 1:8). It is uncertain what those sufferings were. It may have been the riot in Ephesus when Paul preached the gospel in that city, or Paul may be referring to events, unknown to us, in the province of Asia. Because Paul preached the gospel, attempts were made on his life. Paul was in frequent danger from his enemies, both Jews and Gentiles. Paul graphically describes his afflictions (*thlipseos*). As grapes are crushed at the fall festival when the dancers step on them to produce wine, so Paul's sufferings were a crushing experience. Paul was burdened beyond his natural strength. Paul is pictured like an animal would be, sinking under the load of an excessive burden.[10]

The result was that Paul despaired even of life. Paul did not have the personal power to withstand the trials he was experiencing. His despair was extreme, intense. "Life" is emphatic in this verse. Paul's despair was so intense, he despaired even of *life!* How can this be? An apostle of our Lord, suffering to the limits of his endurance?

Sometimes believers experience trials that extend beyond human strength. But that can be valuable. It is a reminder that we do not have the power or inner strength by ourselves to resolve the difficulties we encounter. And that is good; then God can work.

Paul declares, "Indeed, we had the sentence of death within ourselves so that we would not trust in ourselves, but in God who raises the dead" (2 Cor. 1:9). Why does Paul mention "God who raises the dead"? The point is important. If God can do the greater, He can do the lesser. The greatest miracle God can do is raise the dead—and He did precisely that when He raised the Lord Jesus from the dead. Since God can raise the dead, He can resolve any dilemma or difficulty we have. For this reason we must trust Him. In our difficulties we should turn to Him in simple, quiet faith. We must trust Him and not ourselves.

In our human nature we are prone to manipulate and direct the circumstances for our good, but when calamities come that we cannot resolve, it forces us to stop trusting ourselves and begin trusting in the Lord. It is a difficult but vital lesson to learn.

5

How Powerful Is Satan?

Some time ago in Norman, Oklahoma, police encountered an organization called Covenant of the Seventy-Third Demon. Teenagers, seeking to become full-fledged members of that secret fraternity, were asked by its leaders to engage in church vandalism. They were instructed to turn crosses upside down, rip Bibles apart, and ransack church premises, stealing whatever they found of value. The emblems of God were to be destroyed or ridiculed. By doing this, they were told they would "completely release their souls to the prince of darkness," according to news reports.

By their own admission, these teenagers were following Satan and sought to commit crimes against God's people. This raises a question. What is the relationship of Satan to bad things happening to God's people? Is he behind most of these deeds? Many people think so. Certainly Satan is involved in more than just the events that openly carry his name. But perhaps people give Satan more credit than he should have. One pastor vigorously teaches the necessity of house cleansing by entering each room of the house and pronouncing a special formula to rid the house of satanic attack. Is this biblical? Does Satan have that kind of power? A key question remains: how much power does Satan have over God's people?

SATAN'S CHALLENGE

The Book of Job provides valuable insights concerning Satan's authority over God's people and his ability to commit evil acts against them. The book begins with a description of Job: he was "blameless, upright, fearing God and turning away from evil" (Job 1:1). As the family patriarch, Job offered sacrifices for his children, in case they had sinned (v. 5). This was Job's pattern of life. He was a God-fearing man.

The Lord challenged Satan to consider Job—a "blameless and upright man, fearing God and turning away from evil" (v. 8). In reply, Satan launched an attack against Job: "Does Job fear God for nothing?" (v. 9). Satan accused God of surrounding Job, his family, and his belongings with a hedge of protection. Hadn't God blessed him lavishly, with great material wealth? Why shouldn't he worship God? Then came the challenge: "But put forth Your hand now and touch all that he has; he will surely curse You to Your face" (v. 11).

Satan launched a frontal attack. He accused Job of serving God only because of what was in it for him. God's benevolence to Job was obvious. He would be foolish not to worship God. Look what was in it for him. But Satan argued that if Job's wealth was eliminated from him, he would curse God.

SATAN'S LIMITATIONS

To prove that Job worshiped Him with a pure heart and motive, the Lord accepted the challenge, allowing Satan to remove Job's possessions. God said, "Behold, all that he has is in your power, only do not put forth your hand on him" (v. 12). The point is significant: Satan could only do to Job what God allowed. This is an enormously important point to remember. Satan can only do to believers what God allows—not a single thing more. God placed a definite limitation on what Satan could do to Job: "All that he has is in your power" (v. 12). Satan was restricted from touching Job's health or life. He could only touch Job's possessions.

In swift succession, Satan attacked. Using the Sabeans, an Arab Bedouin tribe, he destroyed Job's oxen and donkeys, killing some of his servants as well. At the same time fire fell on Job's sheep and servants, consuming them. Following that, three bands of Chaldeans raided Job's property, stealing his camels and killing the servants. To climax Satan's attack, a mighty desert wind roared down on Job's house, killing his sons and daughters.

RESPONSE TO SUFFERING

Job's response creates the conclusion to Satan's challenge: "he fell to the ground and worshiped" (v. 20). Job realized that he would leave this world as he had entered it—naked (v. 21). But there was no hint of bitterness. Job realized that everything he had in life was a gift from the Lord and it was the Lord's prerogative to take it away. His conclusion? "The Lord gave and the Lord has taken away. Blessed be the name of the Lord" (v. 21).

The significant point is that Satan's charge was false. He challenged the Lord, "Does Job fear God for nothing?" (v. 9). He inferred that Job worshiped God only because of the material blessings he received from the Lord (vv. 9–11). But Satan was wrong. The Lord allowed Satan to remove all of Job's physical blessings—his family (except his wife) and his possessions. Yet "through all this Job did not sin nor did he blame God" (v. 22). Even when the Lord allowed Satan to inflict Job with physical illness, Job's devotion to God did not change.

SATAN'S SECOND ASSAULT

Following Job's loss and his sinless response to his suffering, the Lord reminded Satan, "Have you considered My servant Job? For there is no one like him on the earth, a blameless and upright man fearing God and turning away from evil. And he still holds fast his integrity, although you incited Me against him to ruin him without cause" (Job 2:3). There is a play on words when God reminds Satan that He afflicted Job "without cause," literally, "for nothing." The same phrase, "for nothing," is used in 1:9. The point is clear: Job does serve God "for nothing." He will still worship God even when his life collapses around him. He does not worship God for what God gives him or does for him. He worships God out of a heart of integrity; he worships God because He is worthy of the believer's worship.

Nonetheless, Satan continues his assault on God's servant. He maintains that Job still has not been adequately tested. His life is most valuable to him. "Skin for skin! Yes, all that a man has he will give for his life," challenged Satan (2:4). Satan may have implied that Job would give the skins of his animals, servants, and children for his own skin. More likely, it means that Job would give up everything so that he might save his life.[1] Satan argued that Job would curse God to His face if he would lose his health (v. 5).

GOD'S SOVEREIGN PERMISSION

Once more the Lord permitted Satan to afflict Job, this time by touching his body. So Satan struck Job with pus-filled boils from the bottom of his foot to the top of his head (v. 7). Job's suffering was so severe he removed himself from the community to the town dunghill, the place for dumping refuse. There the patriarch sat and scraped his painful, itching sores (v. 8).

Ironically, Job's wife remained untouched in all the events, perhaps because she was the Adversary's ally. She scolded Job, "Do you still hold fast your integrity? Curse God and die!" (v. 9).

Surely, this solicitation to sin comes from the enemy. When a believer suffers, there will always be those who give the wrong advice, seeking to derail the real purpose for the suffering.

But Job was not deflected. He admonished his wife, "You speak as one of the foolish women speaks. Shall we indeed accept good from God and not accept adversity?" (v. 10). This was indeed a provocative statement—one every believer should ponder. We assume that the blessings of God should naturally come to us; we take them for granted. But when adversity strikes, we think it is unnatural. We ask ourselves, "Why should this happen to me?" Why do we assume that we deserve only goodness and tranquility and that difficulties are unnatural and unwarranted?

Not Job. He understood that both blessing and adversity may come from the same beneficent Lord. But ultimately, Job's response proved Satan wrong: "In all this Job did not sin with his lips" (2:10). God was proven true, and the Lord's servant was vindicated.

WHY WORSHIP GOD?

"Job's amazing response showed Satan was utterly wrong in predicting that Job would curse God. Devotion *is* possible without dollars received in return; people *can* be godly apart from material gain," writes Bible scholar Roy Zuck. "Job's saintly worship at the moment of extreme loss and intense grief verified God's words about Job's godly character."[2] The entire issue of suffering in the Book of Job was resolved in 1:20–22 and 2:10. Job proved that believers will worship God "for nothing."

That's the point. God's people will still worship God when bad things happen. God's people do not worship God because of the material benefits they derive from Him. They worship Him out of adoration because of their redemption in Christ.

When bad things happen to believers, they recognize that the Lord is sovereign. In His infinite goodness and wisdom, He gives and also takes away—for reasons we may never know. But the right response is always the response of Job: "He fell to the ground and worshiped" (1:20). It means we entrust our lives to an all-wise sovereign God and we conclude with Job: "Shall we indeed accept good from God and not accept adversity?" (2:10).

SATAN HINDERS

Today Satan continues to attack believers, hindering them in their spiritual progress and service for the Lord. Paul expressed his sincere desire to see the fledgling Thessalonian believers, yet he exclaimed, "Satan hindered us" (1 Thess. 2:18). Paul does not specifically say how Satan prevented him from traveling to Thessalonica, but he did. Paul's expression of Satan's hinderance is illustrative. The word *hindered* "was originally used of breaking up a road to render it impassable; later it was used in a military sense of making a break through the enemy's line. It was also used in the athletic sense of cutting in on someone during a race."[3]

So Satan hinders believers. But how did he hinder Paul? How does he hinder believers? Paul may be hinting at Satan's hinderance when he says that the Jewish religious leaders hindered him from speaking to the Gentiles (1 Thess. 2:16). In that case Satan hinders by operating through unbelievers. Certainly that is a plausible explanation.

History is filled with events where unbelievers have hindered God's people. The rise of Islam in the seventh century greatly curtailed Christianity, virtually closing North Africa to the gospel. In the past century, atheistic communism viciously opposed the proclamation of the gospel and severely persecuted Christians who attempted to spread the message of Christ. C. Fred Dickason, retired chairman of the department of theology at Moody Bible Insitute, has noted the role of Satan in the affairs of nations:

> Satan uses his angels to influence the affairs of nations, particularly in their opposition to God's program with Israel

or with the church (Daniel 10:13, 20; Ephesians 6:12; 1 Thessalonians 2:18).

Hitler's occult involvement and Stalin's staunch atheism gave Satan great opportunity through their great hatred and murderous actions to destroy many Jews and Christians.[4]

Dickason, an expert in Satan, the occult, and angels, says, "[Satan] would use governmental authorities to hinder the spread of the gospel at home and abroad. . . . certain African nations in their nationalistic programming have been insisting on a return to animistic and idolatrous religions and are persecuting and murdering national Christians and deporting missionaries."[5]

A NORTH AFRICAN FARMER SUFFERS

Ibrahim (not his real name) was a twenty-six-year-old Arab farmer in North Africa. A devoted follower of Jesus Christ, Ibrahim was unashamed of his devotion—he aggressively shared the gospel of Jesus Christ with the Muslim people. Many became upset at Ibrahim's bold evangelism, and one day a mob of men, armed with knives, machetes, spears, and guns, confronted Ibrahim. They were ready to kill him. They had already trashed the round hut where Ibrahim and the other believers worshiped. When men displayed a box of Bibles they had taken from the church, Ibrahim stood up to them. "We're not going to let you burn those books," he exclaimed. The bold believer fearlessly challenged his Muslim enemies. He finally grabbed the box of Bibles and carried them back to the believers. As God would have it, a physical confrontation did not occur.

The town's Islamic council soon convened and held "Islamic court" over them. For three days the believers were challenged concerning their faith in Jesus. One of the Muslim men had stolen a tape with a condensed version of the Bible from Genesis to Revelation—and they played it. The Muslims were listening to the Bible! Yet, at the end, they challenged Ibrahim and his followers: "Will you return to Islam?"

Ibrahim and the other believers immediately responded no. As a result, they were banished from their village, the town, and the entire county. To return was an automatic death sentence. . . . Barred from their homes, the believers and their families survived in ramshackle tents near the country border. . . . With no source of clean water, day-to-day life under the blistering North African sun was brutal.[6]

A year later they were invited to return to their village; instead, they founded a new village a few miles away. But what was the ultimate outcome of the brutality and suffering of these faithful believers? "Today, church members estimate they've shared the gospel with more than 5,000 people. At least 90 have been baptized. Under Ibrahim's leadership, the church itself has grown from a group of 10 to more than 25 and is focused on evangelizing three major tribes."[7]

Even in America, believers have been hindered from proclaiming Christ through legislation interpreted negatively. Under the guise of pluralism, Christians have been thwarted on many fronts in America from spreading the gospel. So Satan hinders believers from spreading the gospel by working through unbelievers.

SATAN'S SCHEMES

We encounter difficulties, opposition, and frustrations, and we think the problem is the person who has created the difficulty for us. Yet Scripture reminds us that "our struggle is not against flesh and blood, but against the rulers, against the powers, against the world forces of this darkness, against the spiritual forces of wickedness in the heavenly places" (Ephesians 6:12). Satan is frequently behind the opposition and difficulties we encounter. (I would caution, however, that we ought not to see a demon behind every bush. There are many other reasons for suffering, as we will suggest later in this book.)

An unbelieving husband may chasten his Christian wife for attending church or being involved in Christian activities, but ultimately it is Satan behind the unbelieving husband who is scheming to prevent the spread of Christian truth through the believing wife.

When I was serving a farming community as pastor, I visited the home of a believing wife with an unbelieving husband. He prohibited her from attending worship services. I recall following him around the farmyard, witnessing to him, challenging him with the claims of the gospel. He smiled at me but argued vigorously against Jesus Christ and the gospel. I left the farm with sadness as the Word of God did not penetrate the hard heart of the farmer.

> Satan also hinders God's people through disunity, a sin that divides the assembly.

Why did he oppose the gospel? It was Satan's way of destroying both the home and the Christian woman's ability to worship and serve God freely.

Satan also hinders God's people through disunity in the church fellowship, a sin that divides the assembly. Paul was quick to warn the Corinthians to forgive the repentant sinning brother and receive him back into the fellowship (2 Cor. 2:10). In failing to do so they would succumb to Satan's schemes (2 Cor. 2:11).

Perhaps this is an area where Satan has been particularly successful. Church splits, party factions, disunity—these have all hurt the cause of Christ, and many Christians have suffered.

Paul warned that "in later times some will fall away from the faith, paying attention to deceitful spirits and doctrines of demons"

(1 Tim. 4:1). What are doctrines of demons? These are false teachings that are brought into the church, deceiving the unsuspecting. The doctrine of demons may take many forms. One example of false doctrine being perpetrated today is the "health and wealth" gospel. These people teach that God wants every Christian healthy and wealthy, and they twist the Scriptures to support their physical appetites. But the errors of this movement are well documented.[8] Satan has deceived many through these false teachings —and the church of Jesus Christ has suffered.

In the face of Satan's opposition, the believer is commanded "to stand firm against the schemes of the devil" (Eph. 6:11). This passage graphically pictures Satan's scheming ways. The term "schemes" is used negatively in extrabiblical literature as "cunning," "deception," and "craftiness." In a neutral sense it is used to mean "to treat methodically" and "to handle according to plan." In its use in Ephesians 6:11, "schemes" pictures a military attack against which the believer must be armed. The attacks are repeated and of incalculable variety, posing a great danger, against which, as Paul soberly declares, the armor of God is the only defense.[9]

Believers can withstand and even withhold Satan's attacks by putting on the full armor of God (Eph. 6:13–20). Sometimes Satan wins the battle against believers, culminating in bad things happening to Christians because they fail to put on the full armor of God. Neglecting a life of faith, meditation in the Word, and prayer may result in Satan piercing the believer's armor, resulting in bad things happening.

SATAN TEMPTS

Satan's primary purpose is to deceive people into sinning, whether believers or unbelievers. He is called "the tempter" (Matt. 4:3). The term "the tempter" depicts his nature. He is continually about the business of tempting people. That is his occupation. He even dared to tempt the Savior, the sinless Son of God (Matt. 4:1).

Ever since Satan tempted Eve in the garden and enticed both Eve and Adam to sin, Satan has continued to solicit people to sin. In the first century church, a fledgling group of believers in Thessalonica lost Paul when persecution forced the apostle to flee the city (Acts 17:5–10). Having spent only a few weeks in Thessalonica (vv. 1–4), Paul became concerned for these new Christians. How were they holding up under the persecution and suffering?

So Paul sent Timothy to encourage them (1 Thessalonians 3:2). Through Timothy, Paul reminded them that believers have been destined for suffering—they shouldn't be surprised (vv. 3–4). Paul's primary fear for the Thessalonians was that "the tempter might have tempted you, and our labor would be in vain" (v. 5). Paul was mindful of Satan, that veritable opponent of the gospel, whose mission is to destroy the devotion of believers through temptation. "He never gives up his sinister efforts," wrote Bible commentator D. Edmond Hiebert. "It is always the devil's aim to entice men to sin and bring them to a fall."[10]

Through tempting believers to sin, Satan has even succeeding in destroying leaders of many ministries. The tragic stories of pastors' indiscretions and immoral conduct has damaged many churches. Too many pastors have fallen through becoming emotionally involved with women they were counseling. The counseling elicited temptation, and the temptation became a solicitation to sin, and when lust responded, the destructive sin took place (James 1:14–15).

In addition to wearing the armor of God through a close relationship with Christ, we need to give no opportunity for the flesh by placing ourselves into tempting situations. The great evangelist Billy Graham has set the example of a lifetime in dealing with temptation. Graham remained discreet throughout his ministry concerning even the possibility of temptation. When staying at a hotel, he would never be seen alone; when entering a hotel room,

Billy Graham remained discreet throughout his ministry concerning even the possibility of temptation.

he always had his male associates enter the room first. As a result of his wisdom and caution, Billy Graham has served the Lord faithfully without falling prey to possible temptation and sin. In contrast, one seminary dean flew with his female associate to an extension site. They lodged at the same hotel, drove together in the car, and dined together without company. It was unwise. It is precisely these kinds of temptations that Satan sets up for believers that can easily culminate in a fall.

Another way Satan trips up believers is through the husband neglecting family responsibilities with his children and especially his wife. One pastor continually neglected his wife. An elder became concerned and, along with another elder, followed the pastor one evening. The pastor went to a single woman's apartment. When the pastor emerged much later that night, the elders confronted him. The pastor's ministry was destroyed, and the work of God and the testimony of Jesus Christ were severely damaged.

Satan tempts people, and when believers ignore the precepts of Scripture, they fall prey to Satan and disastrous things happen.

SATAN DESTROYS

Satan has many names, but the name that particularly reflects his operation is *the destroyer*. In Revelation 9 Satan is seen as the king of the abyss, the bottomless pit. He is the king of the demons, with his operation reflected in his Hebrew name, Abaddon, meaning *destruction*, and his Greek name, Apollyon, meaning *destroyer* (9:11). Satan is a destroyer and he constantly seeks to destroy—ministries, homes, families, and lives.

A young married man with small children was actively

involved in youth work. His marriage floundered so he sought fulfillment elsewhere. On the Internet he began corresponding with an out-of-state married woman. They secretly made arrangements to meet in the young man's home state, and the liaison began. Eventually, the out-of-state woman's husband discovered the affair, and his promiscuous wife had a falling out with the young man. The woman called the young man's wife and the affair was exposed. As a result the young man not only was released from his youth work but his home was destroyed.

Why did these bad things happen? A young man became filled with lust for another woman when Satan tempted him and he yielded to the temptation of the flesh. Satan tempts people in their weakness and when they are not grounded in God, they succumb to the deceiver. Satan tempts people in the area of sexual sins (1 Cor. 7:5) and when they are preoccupied with physical desires, they succumb to sexual activity outside the plan of God.

But Satan not only leads people into immorality, he destroys people through death. He is a murderer. When the unbelieving Jews tried to kill Him, Jesus reminded them: "You are of your father the devil, and you want to do the desires of your father. He was a murderer from the beginning, and does not stand in the truth because there is no truth in him. Whenever he speaks a lie, he speaks from his own nature, for he is a liar and the father of lies" (John 8:44). The Jews' intention to kill Jesus came from Satan himself; he put the plan for murder into their hearts.

Unquestionably, Satan was the source of Herod's murderous plan to kill the infants in Bethlehem (Matt. 2:16). Satan sought to not only kill the little Hebrew children; his intention was to destroy the Messiah Himself.

SATAN DEVOURS

Peter pictures Satan like a ferocious animal prowling around, preparing to devour someone. Peter warns his readers, "Be of sober spirit, be on the alert. Your adversary, the devil, prowls around like a roaring lion, seeking someone to devour" (1 Peter 5:8). Satan is an adversary, an enemy who seeks to destroy the work of God. He will frustrate Christians, endeavoring to hinder their spiritual progress and divert them from the path of righteousness. He will bring disruption when a believer is witnessing to a non-Christian; he will lead a Christian into apathy, making him ineffective in his testimony; he will destroy believers by controlling their minds through unwholesome entertainment, leading them into immorality; he will lead married men and women to lust after other women and men, leading to adultery and home destruction. Bad things happen to God's people when Satan devours unsuspecting Christians, destroying their marriages, homes, and ministries.

Both verbs, *prowls* and *seeking*, are in the present tense, reflecting the continuous activity of Satan in constantly prowling about and continuously looking for people he can devour. Satan never sleeps. He is singularly intent on devouring people.

Is there no resolution to Satan's attacks? Yes, there is. The context reveals the resolution; we are to humble ourselves under the mighty hand of God (1 Peter 5:6). We must not be consumed with anxiety; rather, we must cast all our worries on Him because He cares for us (v. 7). We are to resist Satan, standing firm in our faith amid suffering (v. 9).

It is noteworthy that the warning concerning Satan prowling like a roaring lion is amid suffering. Perhaps this is a reminder that we are more susceptible to Satan's attacks when we experience suffering. Suffering should deepen our trust in the Lord but sometimes it may create doubt, even as Eve doubted the goodness of God in the garden (Gen. 3:1–3).

SATAN HAS LIMITS

We may look at our experiences in life and wish to attribute most of our problems to Satan, but the Word of God is emphatic:

Believers live under the protective care of Jesus Christ. Satan can do nothing to believers except what God allows for our good and for His glory.

Amid the troublesome things that happen to believers, Satan should not be accorded more power than he actually has. There are phenomenal promises to remind the believer that Satan is limited in what he can do to Christians. God promises believers, "The Lord is faithful, and He will strengthen and protect you from the evil one" (2 Thess. 3:3). The believer's protection against Satan is based on the faithfulness of God. The Greek text is emphatic, emphasizing the word "faithful": "*Faithful* is the Lord!" God promises two things; the first is inner, and the second outer. The Lord will brace up, support, and strengthen the believer inwardly against the Adversary. But He will also guard and protect the believer outwardly from Satan. The word "protect" is a common word, a military term, meaning to guard both physically and spiritually.[11] It implies "conflict and armed protection against violent attack."[12] Believers "will be protected from outward assault. . . . It is the constant working of the Lord that secures the inward grounding and outward safety of God's people. . . . They are promised safety 'from the evil one.'"[13]

Another phenomenal promise is given in 1 John 5:18, "We know that no one who is born of God sins; but He who was born of God keeps him, and the evil one does not touch him." In contrast to unbelievers who lie "in the power of the evil one" (v. 19), the evil one cannot touch the believer. What a wonderful promise! What a great comfort!

It is apparent that "He who was begotten of God" refers to Jesus Christ.[14] He is also the One who keeps the believer from the power of Satan. Who is strong enough to protect the believer from Satan? Jesus Christ! The promise is precise. The verb "touch" means "to lay hold of someone in order to harm him."[15] Satan is limited in what he can do to believers. Moreover, the present tense "touch" emphasizes a continuing state, an ongoing situation. Because believers live under the constant umbrella of Christ's protection, Satan is unable at any time to harm believers. This is the promise of God.

GOD IS IN CHARGE

Our sovereign God is in control, and He is sovereign over suffering. Sometimes we can see the reason for the suffering, other times we cannot. Nonetheless, Satan is limited in what he can do. God overrules. God is sovereign.

In *If God Is Good*, Randy Alcorn corrects the misconception of many people: "When asked to name the opposite of God, people often answer, 'Satan.' But that's false. Michael the religious archangel, is Satan's opposite. Satan is finite; God is infinite. God has no equal."[16] And David Jeremiah, in his bestselling book *I Never Thought I'd See the Day!* notes the limits placed on Satan: "We must be knowledgeable about Satan and his determination to destroy us. But that does not mean we should fear him or be intimidated. . . . if we have God in our lives, we have within us more power and more protection than any evil can overcome."[17]

Remember too the promise declared in 1 John: "You are from God, little children, and have overcome them; because greater is He who is in you than he who is in the world" (4:4). The child of God is identified with Christ as an overcomer. Through Christ we have the victory. Through Christ believers are indwelt by the Spirit of God (Rom. 8:9; 2 Cor. 1:22), and the Holy Spirit is greater than Satan.

Bad things happen to God's people when they submit to the authority of Satan, allowing him to deceive them into disobeying the Word of God. Satan can also effect destruction in a variety of ways.

Nonetheless, Satan is limited in his authority and can only do what God allows. God is sovereign over all—including Satan. Therefore, Satan will never thwart the sovereign, all-wise plan of God.

6

How Does Sin Affect
Our Suffering?

Andy, in his midforties, was in the hospital for treatment when I dropped by. His devoted, friendly wife was with him, as was their teenage son. All three are Christians.

Andy explained that he had lung cancer. "This is the result of smoking for thirty years," Andy calmly confided. He wasn't bitter or angry. He simply recognized that his many years of smoking cigarettes had destroyed his lungs. I prayed with Andy and his family and left, but my heart was sad. Here was a middle-aged man with a wonderful family who could have had a great future, enjoying the blessings of a Christian home. Instead, he was facing premature death because of a habit that was detrimental to his health.

The family was on the precipice of great sorrow. Bad things were about to happen to this Christian family.

Everything happens for a reason. Sometimes the reason for bad things in our lives is our own sinful actions. There are primary principles in God's Word that must be observed to avoid having some bad things happen. Sometimes we bring calamities on ourselves because we disobey the injunctions of Scripture—and there are numerous warnings to avoid.

An overarching principle is the biblical admonition: "Do you not know that your body is a temple of the Holy Spirit who is in you, whom you have from God, and that you are not your own? For you have been bought with a price; therefore glorify God in your body" (1 Corinthains 6:19–20).

Clearly, this command has many applications. In this context, Paul is warning the Corinthians about immorality. Do believers need warning concerning immorality? Yes. Tragically, believers sometimes commit sexual immorality, including adultery.

ADULTERY'S IMPACT ON THE CHRISTIAN COMMUNITY

An extramarital affair in a marriage is devastating to both partners. But an affair is equally destructive to churches and other Christian ministries. A certain Bible school years ago was having a profound effect on its community and on the mission field. It was a catalyst in providing leadership in Christian education. Hundreds of young men and women were being trained for ministry. The school exhibited an evangelistic fervor, with students unabashedly sharing their faith in Jesus Christ and winning unbelievers to faith in the Savior. God was prospering the school with its burgeoning enrollment.

One day the president, who had served the school with distinction and longevity, left his wife and ran away with a secretary. The school never recovered. From that moment on the school faltered. Attendance dropped. Support dwindled. Finally, the institution was forced to sell its prime property and relocate to a small, insignificant campus. But even in its new location and reorganization the school failed to develop. It finally closed its doors and is no longer in existence. One adulterous affair destroyed a substantial work of God. Bad things happen—and many Christians can be affected—when believers sin.

Further, who can fathom the fallout from a sin like this? Hundreds of students could be disillusioned concerning their faith, terminating their studies, regressing in their spiritual lives. Because vast numbers of students would not be trained for ministry, fewer graduates would enter the ministry at home and in the mission field. Missions would be affected; evangelism in the foreign fields would suffer . . . The result of a Christian's sin can be extreme in its negative effect.

Sexual misconduct has had a similar impact in many churches and Christian organizations over the years.

DAVID'S ADULTERY

Probably the classic Bible example of bad things happening because of the sin of adultery is King David. David's sin began with several mistakes. At a time when kings went out to war, David elected to stay home (2 Samuel 11:1). David put himself in a vulnerable place when he had little to do and found himself in the wrong place at the wrong time. Walking on the roof of his house in the evening, David saw Bathsheba bathing. Instead of averting his eyes from lust (Job 31:1), he inquired about her. Even though David was informed she was the wife of Uriah, David took Bathsheba and committed adultery with her (2 Sam. 11:4).

One evening of pleasure brought a lifetime of bad things and tragedy upon David, his family, and his nation. David involved others in his sin (v. 15), and ultimately it led to the murder of Uriah (v. 17). But that was only the beginning. Foreign nations heard of it and blasphemed the name of the Lord (12:14); the baby born to Bathsheba died (v. 14). David had trouble with his family (2 Sam. 13–18), particularly with his son Absalom, who rebelled (13:23 ff.). Ultimately, Absalom led a national rebellion against his father and David was forced to flee Jerusalem (2 Sam. 15). Finally, Absalom was killed by Joab, David's general (18:14). Sheba led another revolt against David, but Joab pursued and killed

Sheba—but Joab also killed Amasa, David's new general, because of jealousy (20:10).

David's life was filled with warfare; in fact, it prohibited him from building the Lord's temple. The singular sin of adultery destroyed David's life and brought innumerable bad things not only to David, but also to his family and the nation of Israel.

THE SIN OF IGNORING IMMORALITY

Bad things also affect the entire church when sin is condoned. The Corinthian church had condoned the unbelievable: a man in their midst was living in incest with his stepmother (1 Cor. 5:1). Later the apostle Paul chided them because they had become arrogant about the matter. They were putting up with it; they were accepting it. But Paul had already judged the man as though he were in their midst—he admonished them to remove the man from their church fellowship (vv. 2–3, 7). Condoning immorality in the assembly was like allowing a cancer in the body—it would soon spread to other members.

Such acceptance recurs today among so-called evangelicals. Jacobsen reports, "I actually had a young lady try to convince me there was no contradiction between her claim to be a Christian and her promiscuous lifestyle. 'With all the sexual temptations of our day, God certainly can't expect a single person to be celibate.'"[1]

Some Corinthians may have thought that immorality was a natural appetite like hunger. For that reason they may have believed that immorality was acceptable. Paul vehemently denied this foolish thinking: "The body is not for immorality, but for the Lord" (1 Co. 6:13). The believer's body belongs to the Lord, not to sexual immorality. The body is eternal; it will be resurrected and glorified (v. 14). The believer's body belongs to Christ; it is a member of Christ. How can the body that has been redeemed from sin by the precious blood of Jesus Christ be joined in sexual union to a prostitute (v. 15)? It is unthinkable.

"Flee immorality," Paul warns (verse 18). Immorality (*porneia*) involves both premarital sexual relations as well as adultery. The believer is commanded to flee, to run from immorality. This is to be a constant and habitual fleeing.

Decisions about moral purity are made before the temptation occurs. Joseph didn't decide to flee from Potiphar's wife when she enticed him. That decision had been made long before that. Reason may give way to emotion in the intensity of the temptation. The decision must be made beforehand. A professor wisely warned his students, "Never allow yourself to be alone with a member of the opposite sex. Don't drive in a car alone with a member of the opposite sex. Take another person along." Wise advice.

WHOSE BODY IS IT?

Immorality plagued the church at Corinth. Paul reminded them on several occasions: "Do you not know that you are a temple of God, and that the Spirit of God dwells in you?" (1 Cor. 3:16). "Do you not know that your body is a temple of the Holy Spirit who is in you, whom you have from God, and that you are not your own?" (6:19). The believer's body is a temple of God and a temple of the Holy Spirit.

Certainly Paul's thought reverts to the Old Testament tabernacle where the glory of God dwelt in the temple. The word "temple" (*naos*) identifies the temple as the inner precinct, the Holy of Holies, where the glory of God dwelt with Israel. "The believer therefore does not belong to himself," wrote Bible scholar Robert Gromacki. "His very personality (intellect, emotions, and will), his ambitions and abilities, and his body with all of its desires are not his to command and to please. He totally belongs to His divine occupant."[2]

What are the implications? A couple of things: our body is God's sacred dwelling place; and the Lord is the proprietor of our body.[3] We do not have ownership over it. It belongs to God. Does that determine how we take care of our body? Absolutely. If my body is the temple of God, then I am under obligation to take care of it. I will not abuse it, neglect it, or destroy it through immorality or bad habits.

CARING FOR OUR PHYSICAL BODY

Jim was a seminary professor who loved to study the Scriptures and interact with students. He was highly respected for his depth of knowledge and understanding of the Scriptures and theological issues. It was common to see Jim standing in the hall or sitting at his desk, vigorously discussing keys issues with students.

But Jim had an unusual habit. In the morning he could be seen shuffling toward his office with an eight pack of sixteen-ounce Cokes in one hand and a box with a dozen donuts in the other. He placed the Coca-Cola on the floor beside his desk and the donuts within arm's reach on top of his desk. Throughout the day Jim drank the Cokes and ate the donuts.

He neglected the care of his body and did not keep a proper diet. As a result, Jim was significantly overweight. His obesity led to an early retirement from his ministry and an early death. A brilliant mind with a potential for decades of ministry was curtailed by bad eating habits that ultimately destroyed his body.

Many agree that caring for the temple of God includes looking after our health. When we think of the body as the temple of God, we assume that refraining from tobacco and alcoholic beverages deals with the issue. That's true, but good health includes much more. Obesity, for example, is a serious health problem. A 2010 study reported in the *New England Journal of Medicine* found that women who were obese had an increased risk of early death ranging from 44 to 88 percent compared to healthy woman who never smoked. "Those who were morbidly obese were two times more likely to die prematurely. The results for men were similar."[4]

Problems that plague the overweight person beside diabetes and circulatory issues include arthritis, heart disease, kidney trouble, and premature wear and deterioration of knee and ankle joints. Most significantly, the obese person can die an early death. "As reported in *Nation's Business*, 'If you are overweight by 10 percent, your chances of surviving the next 20 years are 15 percent less than if you had ideal weight; if you are 20 percent overweight, your chances are 25 percent less; if you are 30 percent overweight, 45 percent less.'"[5]

Surely we need to consider weight problems when we acknowledge that our body is the temple of the Holy Spirit. To purposely adopt bad eating habits, to overeat, to eat unhealthy foods, and thereby bring on an early death, is sin. Bad things happen to God's people when they abuse their bodies.

"WHATEVER YOU DO"

In a summary statement, the Scripture directs us: "Whether, then, you eat or drink or whatever you do, do all to the glory of God" (1 Cor. 10:31). In that culture, believers were not to eat meat sacrificed to idols if it became a stumbling block to the weak (1 Cor. 8:8–9). Now Paul broadens the principle. "Whatever" we do, it is to be for God's glory.

This means all things related to the body and mind. It means taking care of our bodies through proper eating and exercise; being financially responsible, paying our financial obligations and living within our income; being careful what we read, listen to, watch on television, and read and see on the Internet. There are many, many applications. But taking care of the body is surely one of them. Another is finances.

CONTROLLING FINANCES

Carol worked for a Christian institution for a salary of only $25,000 per year; but a smooth talking salesman enticed her to

purchase a new car that had a payoff of $29,900. It was a beauti-
ful car, but she couldn't afford the payments. In addition, Carol had
credit card debts of another $20,000. She drove off in the new car
but eventually, unable to cope with these debts, she fell behind in
her payments.

One morning as she was looking out of the window where she
worked, she saw a tow truck driver hitch up her car and haul it
away. Her car was repossessed. She cried as she realized her
dilemma. She saw no resolution to her financial problem so she
decided to file for bankruptcy. But first she went on a shopping
spree—with her credit cards—and the following Monday she filed
for bankruptcy. But now she was without a car, and she had a bad
credit rating.

Bad things were happening to Carol. Why? She brought the
problems on herself because of her failure to live within her
budget. Her low salary did not permit the luxury of a new car. She
should never have gone to the new car showroom to be enticed
by a salesman. She further complicated her problem by buying
things on her credit cards when she knew she wasn't going to pay
for the merchandise she was filing for bankruptcy. Plainly, Carol
was sinning. She herself brought on the bad things that were happening to her.

Probably finances are a major source of problems, even for
Christians. If we are not careful about what we think about or
watch, we will covet material things and be drawn into spending
money we don't have for things we can't afford or don't really
need.

Finances also come under the injunction to do all to the glory
of God. The Lord is dishonored when believers are unfaithful in
their finances. Moreover, debt produces financial bondage, wasted
money on interest payments, and the inability to be actively
involved in supporting the ministries of the church. Bad things
happen to God's people when they live beyond their means and

charge things on their credit cards that they can't afford. Money is one of the major sources of family disruption, quarreling, and divorce.

This bad thing can have a good resolution—but it will take work and sacrifice. When Clara declared bankruptcy, she needed to recognize her obligation in paying her debts. She needed to consult with a financial counselor and determine a method whereby she could repay all her financial obligations, while living within her financial means. As a Christian, this would be her responsibility—and the right way of dealing with the problem that she brought on herself.

HOW A WORLDLY FOCUS HURTS US

The apostle John issues a straightforward command to Christians: "Do not love the world nor the things in the world. If anyone loves the world, the love of the Father is not in him" (1 John 2:15). What is "the world"? "The world" (kosmos) stands for a society that is controlled by Satan and is hostile toward God. It is both a philosophy and a way of life, as well as a tangible, experiential system. It is humanity and everything it represents, in darkness and in rebellion against God.

John explains the reason for the prohibition in the following verse: "For all that is in the world, the lust of the flesh and the lust of the eyes and the boastful pride of life, is not from the Father, but is from the world" (2:16). The threefold phrase "the lust of the flesh, the lust of the eyes and the boastful pride of life" pertain to Satan's deceptive methods of tempting people to sin. This is how he led Eve to sin (Gen. 3:6). The lust of the flesh reflects wrongful desires; the lust of the eyes refers to coveting; the boastful pride of life means pride in what one has or does.

A love of the world promotes materialism, a love and devotion to things. When a believer becomes preoccupied with the world—in whatever form that takes—bad things will happen. A worldly focus may result in marital arguments over finances, which may lead to thoughts of divorce. A worldly focus may result in a spiritual barrenness. There may even be sickness or financial hardship.

A solution to a love for the things in the world is contentment. Scripture reminds us, "But godliness actually is a means of great gain when accompanied by contentment. For we have brought nothing into the world, so we cannot take anything out of it either. If we have food and covering, with these we shall be content" (1 Tim. 6:6–8). Jesus reminds us that life is more than things: "Is not life more than food, and the body more than clothing?" (Matt. 6:25). A preoccupation with the world misses the purpose of our being here.

Jonathan Edwards reminds us: "The end of the creation is that the creation might glorify [God]. Now what is glorifying God, but a rejoicing at that glory He has displayed?"[6] The believer's purpose is to fully enjoy life through glorifying God. What a wonderful insight! How foolishly we miss our created purpose with our intense concentration on temporary things and a world that is passing away.

FAMILY RESPONSIBILITIES

Sin can even lead to suffering among Christian families. Scripture is replete with instruction on raising children. Fathers are to raise their children in the "discipline and instruction of the Lord" (Eph. 6:4). This involves spending time with them, teaching them, guiding them. Mothers are instructed to "love their children, [to be] workers at home" (Titus 2:4b–5). When these commands are ignored, children go astray and bad things happen.

Jan failed to receive proper guidance from her parents and in her desperation married an unbelieving husband. The marriage was broken from the beginning. It wasn't long before her husband began to abuse her, physically beating her. She left her husband,

ultimately divorced him, and brought her children to her parents
to raise. It became a burden for both her and her parents. Bad
things happened. Why? Because the parents failed to train Jan in
righteousness, and failed to guide her in Christian principles. Jan
sinned by marrying an unbeliever (2 Cor. 6:14). Many people suffered for a long time: Jan had a broken home; her children had no
father. Jan's parents were forced to raise small children when they
were older and tired. When they should have found joy in their
grandchildren, they received a burden instead. When God's people
disobey God's Word, bad things happen.

Howard Hendricks was flying from San Francisco to Chicago,
seated next to a young businessman who was an executive with a
small corporation in the Chicago area: "I engaged him in casual
conversation, and when it seemed appropriate I began talking
about spiritual things. The moment I did, he bristled. He said,
'Would you mind if we changed the subject?'

"'Well,' I said, 'I'd be interested to know why.'

"'I'll tell you why,' he said. 'I'm not interested in Christianity
because Christianity robbed me of my parents, and I'm not interested in anything that would do that.'"

The executive began to tell the story of a father who traveled
extensively as a Christian businessman, giving his testimony, and
a mother who was quite active in the community, teaching home
Bible classes. Then the executive added "with a touch of sarcasm
and obvious bitterness," according to Hendricks, "My parents were
so busy leading everyone else to Jesus Christ that they lost their
own four boys, and there's not a one of us that's interested. So
would you mind if we changed the subject?"[7]

Parents fail in raising their children biblically through neglect.
But failure in child rearing may take several forms. Sometimes parents violate God's standard by trying to be a friend to their children instead of a parent. But tragedy may result. Florida Assistant
State Attorney Shirley Williams commented on the parent-teen

problem: "The rules are different now. Parents used to be ashamed if they let their children misbehave and act up. And now they're ashamed to discipline their children."[8]

> Some parents violate God's standard by trying to be a friend to their children instead of a parent.

Many Christian education leaders have observed that we live in a filiocentric society—and parents are literally afraid of their children. As a result, they fail to raise their children according to biblical standards. And bad things happen.

INSTRUCTING CHILDREN

God has given believers clear directives through His Word concerning how Christian parents are to raise their children. Fathers are instructed: "Do not provoke your children to anger; but bring them up in the discipline and instruction of the Lord" (Eph. 6:4). The command is both positive and negative. Negatively, fathers are not to incite their children to anger. "This involves avoiding attitudes, words, and actions which would drive a child to angry exasperation or resentment and thus rules out excessively severe discipline, unreasonably harsh demands, abuse of authority, arbitrariness, unfairness, constant nagging and condemnation, subjecting a child to humiliation, and all forms of gross insensitivity to a child's needs and sensibilities."[9]

Not exasperating one's children requires wisdom and understanding. It means parents become keenly observant of the child's nature and ability at a given age level. Solomon instructs: "Train up a child in the way he should go, even when he is old he will not depart from it" (Prov. 22:6). What does this classic passage mean? It means the parents are observant concerning the child's nature and ability at each age level. It means the father understands what the child can and cannot do at a certain age. It means the parent will not have unrealistic expectations of the child. It means the father will nurture an appetite of the things of God in the child from an early age. It means that when parents are faithful in nurturing their children in the Lord, they have established the child's pattern for life.

The positive command for Christian fathers is to "bring them up in the discipline and instruction of the Lord" (Eph. 6:4). "Discipline" (*paideia*) means the father guides, instructs, and teaches (including reprimanding) the child.[10] Instruction "refers to the training by word—by the word of encouragement, when this is sufficient, but also that of remonstrance, reproof, and blame, where these may be required."[11] Permissiveness is not a biblical perspective in child training.

Training a child toward spiritual maturity in adulthood takes time, observation, prayer, and the applicational instruction of Scripture. Many things can blot out the parents' success in child training—indifference, preoccupation with work or television, or carelessness. But children don't grow to spiritual maturity by accident. It takes time and hard work by parents.

THE SIN OF GOSSIP

Gossip may seem to be a minor sin, but it is a serious sin and causes much pain, even suffering, as people are wrongly maligned. Twice Paul warns women not to be "malicious gossips" (1 Tim. 3:11; Titus 2:3). Ironically, the phrase "malicious gossips" is translated from the Greek word *diabolous*, which is actually a title of Satan, and is normally translated as "Devil" (Matt. 4:1; Eph. 4:27, etc.). As translated, the word means "malicious gossips;" it also means to slander.

As the Devil slanders God's people, so, unfortunately, some Christians slander other Christians—men and women alike.

What does gossip achieve? Disunity. Strife. Division. Church splits. Perhaps there is nothing more harmful to the Lord's work than to create strife and division in a local church. It destroys the Christians' testimony and greatly hinders evangelism and ministry as believers become the object of ridicule in the eyes of the world.

Believers ought to do everything they can to promote unity and harmony in the local church. The tongue, like every member of the human body, must be dedicated to Christ (Rom. 12:1), so that unity may be fostered in the Christian community. Paul is pointed in instructing believers: "Make my joy complete by being of the same mind, maintaining the same love, united in spirit, intent on one purpose" (Phil. 2:2). He also warns, "Be of the same mind toward one another" (Rom. 12:16).

Gossip is the Devil's work that destroys the work of God. As believers we must use our tongues to edify and build up one another so that bad things do not happen to God's people through gossip.

THINKING ON THINGS ABOVE

Scripture is instructive concerning the believer's mind: "If you have been raised up with Christ, keep seeking the things above, where Christ is, seated at the right hand of God. Set your mind on the things above, not on the things that are on earth. For you have died and your life is hidden with Christ in God" (Col.. 3:1–3).

We are exhorted to habitually keep seeking the things above. It is something we do daily, constantly. "Set your mind" is our "outlook on everything."[12] It is how we think. Our minds are occupied with Christ, and the Scriptures direct our decisions through each day. The Word of God affects our attitudes, our motives, our practice.

What are the things above? Ephesians 1:3 reminds us that believers are positionally in the heavenlies, seated together with Christ. We are to seek the things that pertain to Christ—forgiveness, justification, joy, hope, peace, love. These wonderful thoughts are to fill our minds. They are to fully occupy our thinking.

This is similar to Philippians 4:8: "Finally, brethren, whatever is true, whatever is honorable, whatever is right, whatever is pure, whatever is lovely, whatever is of good repute, if there is any excellence and anything worthy of praise, dwell on these things." We are to constantly think about these things. It is to be our habitual, continual practice.

Peter reminds us: "Therefore, prepare your minds for action, keep sober in spirit, fix your hope completely on the grace to be brought to you at the revelation of Jesus Christ" (1 Pet. 1:13). Just as the Oriental traveler tied his robe tight around his waist for unhindered walking, so we are called to control our minds. We are not to be sidetracked, diverted from godly thinking patterns.

Mix the world's philosophy with God's Word, and you can assume the world's value system.

There's the other option; believers can fill their minds with secular thinking independent of God, or even anti-Christian entertainment. What happens then? The mind is diverted away from the Lord and His truth. Thinking becomes confused, mixing the world's philosophy with God's Word. Eventually they can assume the world's value system, which is out of sync with God's Word. Countless bad things result—adultery, divorce, broken homes, rebellious children. Such bad things can be averted through right thinking.

HOW TO TRIVIALIZE GOD

One of the tragic results of Christians being engrossed in television programs and movies that are not suitable for Christians to watch, is the misuse of the Lord's name. It is no longer unusual to hear Christians take the Lord's name in vain: "Oh my G—," "Good L—." Apparently they don't even realize what they are doing—taking the Lord's name in vain. The Bible warns us "not [to] take the name of the Lord your God in vain," noting God's displeasure: "for the Lord will not leave him unpunished who takes His name in vain" (Ex. 20:7; repeated in Deut. 5:11).

This is serious. This is not an incidental matter. We have come a long way from the Old Testament manuscript copyists who would go and wash their hands before they would write the Lord's name and would not pronounce the tetragrammaton, "YHWH." Today when Christians use the texting abbreviation "OMG" or declare aloud "Oh my God," they tell others (and our own minds) that God is simply an expression of surprise.

OBEY THE BIBLE

Obeying God's Word does more than bring us right thinking. It also brings us safety and success. God always looks out for our welfare and has given His Word for our good.

Pete was a good friend of mine when we were students in Bible college. He was a cheerful, likeable man who had a real heart for God and for others. But Pete had a problem: He had a heavy foot when driving his Mercedes. One winter day Pete was heading west along a major highway. With driving snow, blizzard conditions caused extremely poor visibility. But that didn't slow Pete much.

Driving ahead of him at a much slower speed was a truck pulling a load of timber, which protruded from the back. At his high speed Pete ran into one of the poles. Pete was killed instantly. Here was a wonderful, devout Christian—except he flaunted the speed limit law. "Every person is to be in subjection to the governing authorities" declares Romans 13:1. We are to obey the governmental laws.

Pete's defying the speed limit was a transgression of the civil law and God's law as well. Sometimes the consequences of sin can be severe. In this case his rebellion was fatal.

Conversely, obey the law and you will find success. God's Word promises success to the believer through meditating on the Scriptures and obeying them: "This book of the law shall not depart from your mouth, but you shall meditate on it day and night, so that you may be careful to do according to all that is written in it; for then you will make your way prosperous, and then you will have success" (Josh. 1:8). The psalmist also promises success to the godly man who meditates in the Word of God: "His delight is in the law of the Lord, and in His law he meditates day and night. He will be like a tree firmly planted by streams of water, which yields its fruit in its season and its leaf does not wither; and in whatever he does, he prospers" (Ps. 1:2–3).

> God's Word enables us to have good family relations, loving homes, and meaningful relationships.

Suffering comes from sin—disobeying God's Word and His instructions for our good. Probably more problems and difficulties befall us that are due to our sin than we realize. God has given us His Word for a purpose. It enables us to live righteously in a wicked world. It enables us to have good family relations, loving homes, and meaningful relationships with other people.

These things are all possible through obedience to God's Word. But disobedience to God's Word results in bad things happening to God's people.

7

Why Are God's People Persecuted?

At the beginning of the twenty-first century, persecution of Christians was not an isolated incident. In Nigeria, for example, when the governments of several northern states instituted Islamic Sharia law in 2000, severe suffering occurred among Christians. Thirty-six churches were destroyed, pastors were killed, twenty Christians were found in a church building that had been burned down, and at the Baptist Theological Seminary in Kawo, the library, chapel, and classrooms were completely burned down.[1]

Also in 2000, the Muslim government in the Sudan was actively waging war against Christians and Christian ministries. The Sudanese government had dropped bombs on the civilian hospital where Samaritan's Purse was working in the town of Lui. Despite the enormous humanitarian help Samaritan's Purse was providing to Sudanese people at the time, brutality against Christians caused thousands more deaths than in the conflicts in the Balkans.[2]

In Pakistan, two Christian brothers, Rasheed and Saleem

Masih, married men with young children, are now serving thirty-five years in prison for blasphemy because of an incident in 2000. "The charges arose when a vendor refused to serve the Christians ice cream in the same bowls used by Muslims. The vendor later filed a complaint with police, claiming the brothers had made 'bad remarks' against Muhammad and Islam."[3]

KIDNAPPED FOR THEIR FAITH

The story of persecution includes American Christians, of course. In January 1993, three missionary families living in the small village of Pucuro in Panama were busy studying and translating the native language and leading Bible studies. David and Nancy Mankins had been in Pucuro for eight years, studying the Kuna culture and translating Bible lessons into the Kuna language. Rick and Patti Tenenoff, with their three children, had served in Pucuro for six years. Like David, Rick was studying the Kuna Indians and their language. He also was writing a Kuna dictionary and teaching Bible studies to the indigenous people.

A new couple on this mission field, Mark and Tania Rich, had arrived with their two young daughters only recently. The couple were being initiated in their study of the Kuna culture and language. All six missionaries were part of New Tribes Mission (NTM), headquartered in Sanford, Florida.

Then on January 31, their lives changed forever. As J. M. Smith reported:

> On that January day, the three families fell captive to armed Colombian guerrillas who had just seized control of Pucuro. The three missionary men were restrained and bound while their wives were instructed to immediately pack up their clothing. Within minutes, the guerrillas were transferring the men from the village, setting off in the direction of the Colombian border, fifteen miles away.

Dave Mankins, Mark Rich and Rick Tenenoff were never again seen by their families.[4]

Amid the darkness of the event and the years that followed, the families remained strong in their faith, not questioning why the tragedy occurred. Tania Rich remarked, "I think God is doing this for a good reason so that more people will come to know Jesus." Her eight-year-old daughter added, "If Daddy doesn't come home, we will keep on trusting Jesus. If he has been taken to heaven, someday we will see him there."[5]

On October 6, 2001, a memorial service was held for the three missionary families in central Florida, not far from the NTM headquarters. Earlier NTM had announced that a guerrilla group, the Revolutionary Armed Forces of Colombia (FARC), had killed the three men and that the missionaries' bodies may never be found.[6]

TWO FUNDAMENTAL QUESTIONS

These four recent examples of persecution in the worldwide church raise two fundamental questions. First, is persecution a recent or historical phenomenon, something any believer past or present could face? Second, if everything happens for a reason, why does God permit persecution of His people when they do good and present the good news of Christ's love and God's forgiveness?

PERSECUTION FOR TWO MILLENNIA

To our first question, "Is persecution an historical phenomenon that continues today?" we can answer with a resounding yes. History details the persecution against believers for their faith in Jesus Christ. From the persecutions of the early believers recorded in the Book of Acts to the twenty-first century, believers in Christ have suffered for their faith.

Persecution was even committed by well-meaning Christians.

During the Reformation the Anabaptists endured many hardships from both Catholics and Protestants in the Lutheran and Reformed traditions. For their refusal to baptize infants and to attend and financially support the state church, Anabaptists were severely punished. In Switzerland persecution was especially fierce. Believers "were fined, imprisoned, and occasionally sent to the galleys . . . their property was confiscated, and their children declared illegitimate, and incapable of entering into their inheritance; they were branded and whipped into exile; and if they returned, as sometimes they did, they were threatened with the death penalty. Finally upon death, they were denied burial in the common burying grounds."[7]

WHY?

These believers willingly suffered for the truth of Scripture. They considered the truth of God's revelation sufficiently valuable that they would give up their lives to preserve the truth. Few of these believers compromised or recanted, even though they were tortured, lost all their earthly possessions, were driven from their homes, and put to death. They were "men of whom the world was not worthy" (Heb. 11:38).

Some of God's people have been willing to give up personal comfort and even their very lives to preserve God's truth for their day and for successive generations. We owe a debt to those people. Had they not given their lives to preserve the truth, we might be living in darkness today.

The Scriptures tell us followers of Jesus will continue to suffer until Jesus returns. (See, for example, Rom. 8:7; 2 Tim. 2:3; 1 Peter 4:12–14.)

But the more fundamental question is, why does such persecution come? If everything happens for a reason, why does God permit persecution of His people? Both godly leaders and everyday followers devoted to Christ suffer persecution.

BRINGING HONOR TO CHRIST

When the Colombian guerrilas kidnapped Mark Rich and two other missionaries, Tania Rich said of their capture, "I think God is doing this for a good reason so that more people will come to know Jesus." That is *a key reason God's people suffer persecution—so that in their godly response they may bring honor to Christ's name and cause others to turn to Christ for comfort and peace.*

In the mid 1950s five young men and their wives devoted themselves to bringing the gospel of Christ to the fierce Auca people who had resisted all attempts of evangelism. On January 3, 1956, the missionary men established a beachhead named "Palm Beach" in Auca territory in the jungles of Ecuador. Flying over the nearby huts, the missionaries gestured and shouted to the Aucas, inviting them to visit their camp. Three days later, one Auca man and two women approached the camp. Jim Elliot welcomed them, taking them by the hand and leading them to the camp. The Aucas remained at the camp for a day, then disappeared into the jungle.

Two days later, on January 8, more Aucas came to the beach rendezvous to meet the missionaries. Their visit, though, was hostile. Armed with spears, they killed all five missionaries at Palm Beach.[8]

Attempts to contact the men via base radio failed. When a search party set out for the camp, they found the men, their spear-riddled bodies on the beach and floating in the river. Five wives had suddenly become widows; children had lost their fathers.

FIVE MARTYRS WITH A LASTING IMPACT

What was the outcome of those lost lives in Ecuador? At Bible college campuses and in the greater Christian community, the story of the men's willingness to risk death caused many to volunteer for missions service. Others read the feature story in the January 30, 1956, issue of *Life* magazine and were spurred to new devotion to Christ. Jim Elliot's words, found in his personal journal, moved many to consider their own commitment: "He is no fool who gives what he cannot keep to gain that which he cannot lose."[9] His widow, Elisabeth Elliot, chronicles the immediate results:

> To the world at large this was a sad waste of five young lives. But God has His plan and purpose in all things. There were those whose lives were changed by what happened on Palm Beach. In Brazil, a group of Indians at a mission station deep in the Mato Grosso, upon hearing the news, dropped to their knees and cried out to God for forgiveness for their own lack of concern for fellow Indians who did not know of Jesus Christ.
>
> Off the coast of Italy, an American naval officer was involved in an accident at sea. As he floated alone on a raft, he recalled Jim Elliot's words (which he had read in a news report): "When it comes time to die, make sure that all you have to do is die." He prayed that he might be saved, knowing that he had more to do than die. He was not ready. God answered his prayer, and he was rescued. In Des Moines, Iowa, an eight-year-old boy prayed for a week in his room, then announced to his parents: "I'm turning my life over completely to the Lord. I want to try to take the place of one of those five."[10]

But much more than that has transpired. The gospel has penetrated the Auca community (the Aucas are now called Waorani). The widows returned, learned the Auca language, and eventually contacted the natives and brought them the gospel. They responded to the gospel. Minkayi and Kimo, men who had participated in the killing of the missionaries, were among the converts. The New Testament has been translated into their language; many have learned to read the Scriptures. The gospel has come to the Waorani in all its power.[11]

Was this persecution unto death worth it? Forty years later, Jim Elliot's widow would write, "Who of the five men . . . could ever have imagined the long-term effects of their simple act of obedience? They faithfully followed the Master. They paid the ultimate price. Those around the world who have been transformed by their testimony cannot be counted."[12]

THE FIRST MARTYR

So persecution to the point of death is a powerful way some believers will bring honor to His name and that of His Son. Bringing honor to Christ by giving Jesus credit and bringing others to salvation in His name began with the early followers in His church. Stephen was one of the first deacons chosen to serve the early church. This great servant of God, "full of grace and power" (Acts 6:8), debated with the unbelieving religious leaders. When they were unable to cope with his wisdom, they falsely accused him of blasphemy and incited the people against him. With their accusations they succeeded in bringing him before the Sanhedrin, the religious supreme court in Israel.

The Lord empowered Stephen, who traced Israel's history, showing the religious leaders that their history was one of constantly rejecting and persecuting God's servants (Acts 7:1 ff.). When Stephen concluded his sermon, he pointedly reminded them that, when they rejected Jesus as the Messiah, they were acting just like their forefathers (v. 51).

Upon hearing this, the leaders became enraged, and in a mob frenzy, rushed at Stephen, dragged him out of the city, and began to stone him. Understanding Stephen's words as blasphemy, they cried out in rage, covering their ears so they wouldn't hear any more of his "blasphemous" words.

Stephen is the first recorded Christian martyr. For his boldness in proclaiming Jesus as the Messiah and for confronting the unbelieving religious leaders, Stephen was stoned to death.

But the story did not end there. One of the witnesses to Stephen's death, Saul, would begin his own persecutions of Christians (Acts 8:1–4). He became an enemy of the gospel and a fierce persecutor of Christians. But what was the result? "And on that day a great persecution began against the church in Jerusalem, and they were all scattered throughout the regions of Judea and Samaria, except the apostles" (Acts 8:1b). What had the Lord instructed the disciples? To carry the gospel to Jerusalem, Judea, Samaria, and the world (Acts 1:8). The believers were slow in responding to the instruction, so the Lord used persecution for the benefit of the gospel! The believers spread throughout the Roman Empire, carrying the gospel throughout the known world—and the Book of Acts details the spread of the gospel. Persecution had a positive effect.

> Stephen was stoned to death. But the story does not end there.

And what about Saul? Eventually Christ Himself would confront the man who "was in hearty agreement with putting [Stephen] to death" (8:1; cf. 9:3–6). Saul would become known as Paul, the great missionary to the Gentiles (13:9), starting churches across Asia Minor. Soon he would willingly endure persecution. No doubt Paul had heard Stephen's final, godly words of forgiveness: "Lord, do not hold this sin against them!" (7:60) The unjust, seemingly senseless death of Stephen was used for good by God.

SATAN'S ROLE; SATAN'S GOAL

We cannot always understand suffering and death caused by persecution, but we do know one source of persecution. The Adversary will always oppose the gospel—and persecution results. *The second reason for persecution is Satan's role as the Adversary.*

From time immemorial, those who have stood for God's truth have been opposed. Harrassment, ridicule, loss of property, removal from one's homeland, and death—all of these bad things have happened to God's people throughout history. And they will continue to happen when God's servants take a stand for the truth and against error and evil. The Adversary will provoke his own people to oppose the gospel, and as a result Christians will suffer. Satan is active, and his goal remains to undermine Christ's victory by keeping men and women out of God's kingdom.

The Devil's plan can be clearly seen in how he caused people to persecute Jeremiah. God had sovereignly consecrated him, setting him apart to the prophetic ministry (Jer. 1:5). But it was a difficult ministry, which the Lord foretold would occur. The Lord commanded Jeremiah to "speak to them all which I command you. Do not be dismayed before them . . . they will fight against you, but they will not overcome you, for I am with you to deliver you" (vv. 17, 19). Jeremiah received an unusual ministry from the Lord. He commissioned Jeremiah to go to the people and proclaim the Word of God to them—but the Lord reminded the prophet that they would not respond to him! Later, the Lord warned Jeremiah of the commission and consequences of his ministry: "You shall speak all these words to them, but they will not listen to you; and you shall call to them, but they will not answer you" (7:27).

Thankfully, few of us have that kind of a commission. Yet, wherever the gospel is faithfully preached, there will be opposition and persecution. Satan, the Evil One, prods his followers to do so.

Jeremiah warned the people of Judah about judgment because of their sins. Hearing the warning, the people only intensified their opposition to the prophet. In his hometown, the people sought to kill him (11:21). Jeremiah became so discouraged he begged the Lord to take vengeance on his persecutors. He prayed that the Lord would preserve his life because of the reproach he was experiencing for the Lord's sake (15:15). "In effect he was saying: 'O Lord, you are surely aware of what is going on. Take active notice of me in my plight and obtain satisfaction from my persecutors for my sake. Do not be inactive but act now on my behalf, for it is for your sake that I am suffering their rebuffs.'[13]

God indeed does take note of His servants when they are undergoing persecution—and He does act on their behalf. However, He does not always act in the way we expect. Nor is the outcome always like we expect. But God is sovereign and wise in all His ways. Everything happens for a reason.

Probably there is no place as lonely as the ministry. Jeremiah felt himself alone, and in his loneliness he experienced severe opposition. His thinking became twisted, and he complained to the Lord.

> *O Lord, you have deceived me and I was deceived; You have overcome me and prevailed. I have become a laughingstock all day long; Everyone mocks me. For each time I speak, I cry aloud; I proclaim violence and destruction, because for me the word of the Lord has resulted in reproach and derision all day long. (20:7–8)*

It is noteworthy that when suffering for the gospel we can come to faulty conclusions. Our focus may turn on ourselves, on our suffering, and we begin to blame God. *After all*, we tell ourselves, *isn't He all-powerful? Doesn't He have the strength to resolve my dilemma? Of course. Then why doesn't He do something?* And we blame God for our suffering. Is there a reason?

Satan desires that we would compromise our message and, in so doing, our integrity.

But we don't have the big picture. Our vision is too nearsighted. We see only our own needs, and our bodies and emotions cry out for a pain-free life, for tranquility. But God is dealing with the larger picture; He has purposes that we cannot begin to fathom. There is a purpose that far surpasses our comprehension, and we must walk by faith, not sight. We must trust that an all-wise, all-good God is doing what is right and what is best. Yes, there is a reason.

Satan desires that we would give up, compromising our message and, in so doing, our integrity. Significantly, although he complained to the Lord about being deceived, although he was ridiculed for his message, Jeremiah retained his integrity. Surely the prophet was tempted to water down the message to make it more palatable to the people so persecution would be averted. But what was Jeremiah's response? Jeremiah contemplated: "But if I say, 'I will not remember Him or speak any more in His name,' then in my heart it becomes like a burning fire shut up in my bones; and I am weary of holding it in, and I cannot endure it" (v. 9).

> Christian history is rich with the accounts of those who stood true to the Word of God despite the cost.

Despite the oppressive persecution, the prophet did not compromise his message. If he attempted to maintain silence and avoid speaking God's Word to the people, it became like a burning fire within him that had to be released. He could not remain silent; he had to speak God's truth, despite the consequences. What a valuable lesson for everyone enduring persecution for the sake of the gospel. There can be no compromise, no softening of the Savior's message. Thankfully, Christian history is rich with the accounts of men and women who stood true to the Word of God despite the cost. Compromise is never an option amid persecution.

Persecution can taken unusual forms. Satan today has used the pressures of modern society to try to conform us to worldly standards (see Romans 12:2). The politically correct society of America has wrapped its tentacles around the religious community. "Is Jesus the only way to God?" society asks. "Surely there is merit in other religions; surely they also are a road to heaven! Please be tolerant and accept others' viewpoints." Pressure and public ridicule are not uncommon when believers stand firm on the exclusiveness of the Christian message. Epithets of "radical right wing," "woodenheaded fundamentalists," "narrowminded" are among the attacks against Christians. Slander and public derogatory remarks are hurled at evangelicals. Reputations are ruined and the work of God is stifled because of persecution through vilification.

Ridicule, doubt, and direct lies have always been Satan's tools, from the garden of Eden—"You surely will not die! . . . You will be like God, knowing good and evil" (Gen.3:4–5)—to Calvary itself: "He saved others; He cannot save Himself. . . . He trusts in God, let God rescue Him now" (Matt. 27:42–43).

A TIME TO BE FAITHFUL

There is *a third reason that persecution comes into our lives. Persecution gives an opportunity to both develop our faith and to prove our faithfulness.*

Scripture is clear that suffering (i.e., persecution) helps believers develop spiritually. Paul reminds us that we can "exult in our tribulations, knowing that tribulation brings about perseverance; and perseverance, proven character; and proven character, hope; and hope does not disappoint, because the love of God has been poured out within our hearts through the Holy Spirit who was given to us" (Rom. 5:3–5).

How do we experience the love of God? How do we develop proven character and hope? Through suffering. It matures us.

Similarly, the apostle James writes that we should "Consider it all joy. . . when you encounter various trials, knowing that the testing of your faith produces endurance. And let endurance have its perfect result, so that you may be perfect and complete, lacking in nothing" (James 1:2–4). While we may not welcome suffering and persecution when they come our way, we should nonetheless recognize they develop within us spiritual maturity.

For Jeremiah, the persecution gave him opportunity to prove himself faithful to the Lord. The intense opposition to the prophet brought death threats.

Both the priests and the prophets rejected Jeremiah's harsh message from God: repent; otherwise the Lord would destroy Jerusalem, making it a curse to the nations (Jer. 26:1–6). The religious leaders and people seized Jeremiah and demanded the death sentence: "You must die!" (v. 8). Then the priests and the other prophets brought Jeremiah to the New Gate in the temple and formally charged Jeremiah before the officials of the highest tribunal demanded the death sentence (v. 11).

Because Jeremiah warned the people to submit to Babylon, they considered him a traitor to Israel and sought his death. Jeremiah saw their greater need—repentance concerning idolatry and submission to the Lord's discipline for correction. But since Jeremiah was misunderstood, he was persecuted. Worldly people will rarely understand God's servant and will willingly libel the faithful servant with treacherous charges.

Significantly, the threat of death did not silence Jeremiah's proclamation. "The Lord sent me to prophesy against this house and against this city . . . Now therefore amend your ways and your deeds and obey the voice of the Lord your God." (vv. 12–13). Their persecution only proved Jeremiah's faithfulness as he spoke up for God.

TOSSED INTO JAIL

Modern persecutions continue in the pattern of biblical persecutions. Opposition to the gospel has not changed, whether it is prohibiting a child from reading a Bible story in a public school or whether it is persecution of an ancient prophet. Jeremiah the prophet remained faithful to his difficult commission. But opposition to Jeremiah intensified. When the prophet attempted to go to Anathoth and buy a field, he was accused of treason and he was "shut up in the court of the guard" (Jer. 32:2). After Jeremiah was released, he continued his faithful ministry, warning the people not to trust in Egypt; the Babylonians would definitely come and attack Jerusalem. Charging Jeremiah with going over to the Babylonians, they beat the prophet and thrust him into prison (37:15). But Jeremiah continued to preach, warning the people of impending judgment. So King Zedekiah turned Jeremiah over to the officials, who threw the prophet into a cistern where he sank into the mud (38:6).

The history of Jeremiah is one of persecution and suffering. Why did all these bad things happen to Jeremiah? Clearly, persecution resulted because of Jeremiah's faithful proclamation of the Word of God. Satan has always opposed God's Word and he will continue to do so. He operates through people who will oppose God's Word.

JOY IN TRIBULATION

When Paul came to Thessalonica, the unbelieving Jews became jealous, took some wicked men from the public square, and, forming a mob, converged on the believers and dragged them before the public authorities. The entire city and the authorities were in an uproar because Paul had preached the gospel and some had believed (Acts 17:5 ff.). That was the Thessalonian believers' initiation into Christianity!

But what was their response? They "received the word in much tribulation with the joy of the Holy Spirit" (1 Thess. 1:6). The Thessalonian believers had two contrasting experiences: tribulation and joy. Certainly these are seemingly incompatible, yet the believers experienced both. They welcomed the Word of God.

When they heard Paul proclaim the glorious riches in Christ, they responded by receiving the eternal word with intense joy. It was a supernatural joy, the joy of the Holy Spirit.

The moment they became believers, the Holy Spirit indwelt them, filling them with joy. As Bible commentator Edmond Hiebert wrote, "The Spirit was not only the external giver but also the internal source of their joy. No other explanation for their deep joy under the circumstances was possible. A joy arising out of a spurious religious excitement will fail under such circumstances. This experience of 'affliction with joy' was an anomaly to the non-Christian world; it was completely baffling."[14]

This is a fourth reason for persecution, that joy may abound in the midst of great tribulation. We can regard any trial, including persecution with joy (James 1:2); such joy of the Lord can sustain us. In trials, "the joy of the Lord is your strength" (Neh. 8:10).

Remember, the believers experienced "much tribulation" (1 Thess. 1:6). This is graphic. The word "tribulation" (*thlipsis*) means "oppression, affliction, tribulation" and is used "of distress that is brought about by outward circumstances."[15] The word *thlipsis* was used to describe the crushing of grapes in the fall grape harvest. The crushing of the grapes graphically illustrates the stress and pressure of tribulation. The tribulation the believers experienced was intense and severe. Yet through the power of the Spirit, they could respond with joy.

"It was in this double experience that the Thessalonians became imitators of . . . the Lord,"[16] Hiebert notes. What a phenomenal truth! When the believers experienced *both* suffering and joy in the Holy Spirit, they became imitators of the Lord. Surely those are great words of encouragement.

What is your circumstance today? Are you suffering for the cause of Christ? Are you being ridiculed or ostracized because of your faith in Jesus? Let these words comfort and encourage you— you are walking in the Savior's steps. No one suffered like the Lord

> You may have the peaceful joy of Jesus Christ while you are suffering for Him.

Jesus Himself, yet He maintained the joy of the Holy Spirit amid the sufferings. That can be your experience as well. You may have the peaceful joy of Jesus Christ through the Holy Spirit's power while you are suffering for Him.

It is a paradoxical truth that as believers we are called to rejoice in the glorious blessing of our relationship with Jesus Christ and the glory that awaits us, and yet we also rejoice in our sufferings. Paul states, "We exult in hope of the glory of God. And not only this, but we also exult in our tribulations," which bring about perseverance (Rom. 5:2–3). The statement is strong. "Exult" (*kauchometha*) means "a triumphant, rejoicing confidence—in God."[17]

This does not mean the believer looks forward to suffering or rejoicing *for* tribulations as they come, but he rejoices *in* tribulations because of what they do for him spiritually. He rejoices in afflictions "because they humble him and prevent him from having confidence in himself, so that he trusts in God only, and gives glory to him (cf. 2 Cor. xi. 30)."[18] The sufferings of God's people do not overthrow the reality of God's blessings in Christ, "but they are themselves occasions for joyful boasting! The believer should exult 'in' the afflictions themselves, 'to view them as a basis for further confidence in our redeemed status.'"[19]

PERSECUTION TODAY

We began this chapter with accounts of churches being destroyed, seminaries losing libraries and classrooms to fires, even of two Christians being imprisoned for thirty-five years for alleged blasphemy against Muhammad and Islam. But persecution seemingly has intensified, leading not just to suffering, but often death.

In countries where Islam is dominant (e.g., Iran, Indonesia, Saudi Arabia, Pakistan, Sudan, Egypt) and the remaining communist countries (especially China, Vietnam, North Korea, Cuba), persecution of Christians has been severe.

But persecution continues in many other nations as well— India, Nepal, Sri Lanka, Bhutan, Burma, Cambodia, and Mongolia. Books have been written, detailing the fierce persecution and murder of Christians and the destruction of church buildings.[20]

GOOD OUT OF BAD

We look at the suffering of God's saints, from imprisonment to torture and even death, and we often see little good from such suffering. Yet we must always remember: God is sovereign, He is wise, and He is good. Because this is true, good must ultimately come from the suffering. But we may never comprehend it *in our lifetime.* But always there is a reason (sometimes *reasons*).

At times, in hindsight, we can see God's purpose in suffering. Born in 1628, John Bunyan was an unbeliever when he married Margaret Bentley, a Puritan. But influenced by the Puritan preaching, Bunyan experienced a Christian conversion. Soon he became a leader of a congregation in Bedford and a prominent preacher among the Puritans. In 1660, the government announced that all church services apart from the Church of England were illegal. When Bunyan persisted in preaching, he was imprisoned in 1660 in Bedford county jail. There he stayed for twelve years.

Although a bad thing had happened to a man of God, great good came out of it. There was a reason: a book, *The Pilgrim's Progress*, written amid intense persecution, has been in print for over three hundred years and has inspired millions of people. It remains one of the bestselling books of all time.

God in His wisdom and sovereignty will use bad events for good. God can take an imprisonment and use it for good with the wide dissemination of the gospel through writings like *The*

Pilgrim's Progress. Or God may fan the flames of evangelism through the suffering church in China. God is not restricted—nor has He abdicated His sovereignty. He still brings good out of bad, even though we may not recognize it or understand it—but there is a reason. The larger picture may not be seen in our lifetime, restricting us from understanding the suffering. But good must ultimately prevail because God is sovereign and He is also good.

AN UNEXPECTED OUTCOME

Similarly, Paul and Silas were beaten with rods and thrown into prison after Paul cast an evil spirit out of a slave girl (Acts 16:16 ff.) The outcome of their suffering was unexpected.

While in prison, their feet were fastened in stocks that forced their legs wide apart in a torturing position, causing great discomfort and cramping pain.[21] Yet their response was noteworthy: "About midnight Paul and Silas were praying and singing hymns of praise to God, and the prisoners were listening to them" (Acts 16:25). Notice that the response of these two followers of Christ provoked a specific response among others in the jail: "The prisoners were listening to them." Why? Because normally the prisoners would have heard those who had been beaten and tortured crying out with curses against the Romans authorities and against God. Instead, Paul and Silas were praying and singing hymns of praise to God! The joy of the Lord was their strength (see Neh. 8:10). The comment about the prisoners indicates they were amazed at the response of Paul and Silas. These disciples' witness impressed the other prisoners—and led to the spiritual salvation of the jailer himself (Acts 16:28–33.)

SUPERNATURAL GRACE

Perhaps God allows bad things to happen to believers under persecution so they will be a testimony to unbelievers. Ultimately, if there is no difference between believers and unbelievers in suffering, what is the point of being a Christian? A Christian *should* be different in suffering. Believers *should* reflect the grace of God in their lives in difficult times. Perhaps that is precisely the witness that God uses to draw unsaved people to Himself. Why was the Reformation not stamped out through persecution? Why was the Anabaptist movement not destroyed when its people were beaten, tortured, and executed? Why has the church in China not died after having been severely persecuted since 1948? Because God uses the persecution of Christians as a powerful witness to His grace to draw unbelievers to Himself.

The suffering saints have often been the encouragement for others to step forward, having counted the cost, and to be identified with a suffering Savior and with those suffering saints. That is precisely what happened when Paul was imprisoned in Rome. Other believers received encouragement to speak the gospel without fear when they saw Paul's courage in prison (Phil. 1:14).

Perhaps you are suffering for the cause of Christ. You may be ridiculed, ostracized, even to the point of suffering financially and socially—even physically. You may be the only family member who is a believer, and as a result your family may reject you. But there is a divine purpose in it all. God makes no mistakes, neither has He lost control. God directs all the circumstances for His glory and for our good. In persecution His name is glorified and the gospel is extended because believers reflect the supernatural grace of God in their lives. Indeed, there is a reason.

HEAVEN'S PERSPECTIVE

Persecution, even to the point of death, can be explained for all four reasons in this chapter, but no matter the reason, the final outcome should always give us hope. Scripture gives us the larger picture—from God's perspective. Although the religious leaders viewed Stephen's words as blasphemy, the Lord Jesus Himself welcomed Stephen into heaven.

If only we could glimpse into heaven, to see the divine, eternal perspective of the earthly tragedy. That is the focus we must maintain. That is the only true focus, the eternal one. The earthly sufferings—the bad things—form only the partial picture. The final story is told in glory and the believer's joy in the presence of the Savior for all eternity.

We will never have the final answer here. We can only understand that everything happens for a reason when we see it from heaven's perspective.

COURAGE IN DEFENDING THE TRUTH

Amid opposition, amid the stress of faithfully proclaiming God's truth, God's servants must determine to be faithful. Opposition in the Western world may not come from physical violence, but it will come in other ways. The tolerance mode places pressure on Christians. Dr. Albert Mohler, president of the Southern Baptist Theological Seminary in Louisville, Kentucky, has courageously (and graciously) defended the truth of the Scriptures amid considerable opposition. Appearing on public television, questioned and challenged by hostile opponents, Mohler has graciously but faithfully and firmly stood for biblical truth. He has received verbal abuse, even from those who take the name of Christ. Mohler fulfills the same biblical injuction to be approved by God, not to proclaim men-pleasing messages.[22]

Perhaps this is where believers in Christ will be signficantly challenged in the future. The Adversary attacks the bedrock of our Christian beliefs. For instance, who will defend the biblical Jesus? Persecution in the form of ridicule over belief in a literal interpretation of the Bible and the fundamentals of the faith will abound. But amid the ridicule and persecution, believers must determine to please God, not men. Do you and I consider it a privilege to suffer bad things for the sake of the gospel? The future and continuance of biblical Christianity depends on it.

8

Why Suffer for the Gospel?

A young man sensed God's call to the mission field in South America. Having prepared himself for ministry through training, the day of parting from his widowed mother came. It was difficult, but his mother, as a believer, recognized God's call on his life. On his way to South America, he changed planes in Miami and, having a few free moments, decided to scribble a quick note to his mother. Since he had no note paper, he quickly wrote a brief message to his mother on a torn piece of newspaper, mailed it, and boarded his plane for South America. Tragically, the plane crashed en route, killing all on board.

The airlines solemnly notified the widowed mother of the young missionary's death. A day or two later, the mother received her son's note that he mailed from Miami. As she read his note, she noticed it was written on a newspaper article entitled, "Why?"

A QUESTION ASKED FOR CENTURIES

The singular question "Why?" profoundly expressed the grieving widow's thoughts. Why did her son die? Why did this young missionary, dedicated to Jesus Christ, have to lay down his life when he could have done so much for the Lord? Why?

This is a question many people have asked over the centuries. This question is especially difficult when the people who have died have been committed to serving the Savior. Why did these dedicated believers die? Couldn't they have made an impact for Christ? Recall the words of Elisabeth Elliot, the widow of Jim Elliot, one of the five young missionaries slain on a beach in Ecuador as they tried to present the gospel. She admitted, "To the world at large this was a sad waste of five young lives."

AN ETERNAL PERSPECTIVE

But that was not her opinion, nor those of the five men willing to give their lives. Without question, these servants of Christ had an eternal perspective. They would say with Paul, "I do not consider my life of any account as dear to myself, so that I may finish my course and the ministry which I received from the Lord Jesus, to testify solemnly of the gospel of the grace of God" (Acts 20:24).

While many do not understand this, those who are committed to Christ stand ready to suffer for Him, whatever the cost. It may involve financial hardship, separation from family and friends, living in a strange culture, deprivation from the western standard of living, sickness, and, yes, even death itself.

MARTYRS IN AFGHANISTAN

Modern martyrs in Afghanistan died at the hands of ten Taliban gunmen on August 5, 2010. The gunmen opened fire on the Christian workers, killing ten workers with the International Assistance Mission, a humanitarian agency serving in Afghanistan since 1966. The attack took place after members of the IAM medical team had successfully crossed a river swollen by heavy rains. The team rested from the crossing and readied to resume their journey to Kabul, the nation's capital. During that break, the attack came, as described in an Associated Press report:

> The gunmen rushed in, firing bullets over the medical team members' heads. "What's happening?" Tom Little [an optometrist from New York] shouted.
>
> A gunman struck Little in the head with the butt of an AK-47 rifle. Little fell bleeding to the ground. When he tried to get up, the attackers fatally shot him in the torso.
>
> Two of three female members of the team had jumped inside one SUV to hide. The attackers tossed a grenade at the vehicle, killing them both. Then, one by one, they killed the rest of the group—except the driver.[1]

Six Americans, two Afghans, a German, and a Briton were killed.

Why had the Americans gone to Afghanistan? Glen Lapp, a trained nurse from Lancaster, Pennsylvania, and one of the victims, reported to the Mennonite Central Committee: "Where I was, the main thing that [expatriates] can do is to be a presence in the country. Treating people with respect and with love and trying to be a little bit of Christ in this part of the world."[2]

A senseless killing of ten compassionate Christians who sought to help poor Afghans with medical and dental needs. Was there a reason for this tragedy that Christians can understand? One day we may see good come out of this tragedy. But perhaps we may not see it. We may not understand the reason for this until we get to glory.

GAINING THROUGH LOSING

Jesus spoke of this perspective of surrendering our comforts—to face ridicule, rejection, and even risk death—when He said, "Whoever wishes to save his life will lose it; but whoever loses his life for My sake will find it" (Matt. 16:25). The one who wants to "save his life" is the one who compromises his life in this world. To be at peace with everyone and enjoy acceptance with everyone, this person gives up his identification with Christ. The one who has lost "his life for My sake" is the one who willingly suffers ridicule, rejection, and ostracism for his identification with Christ. He forfeits his social position, his prestige, the good life of this world, to be identified with Christ in rejection, humiliation, and suffering. But he finds true life, both in this life and in the future life. He has an eternal perspective.

During the pregame portion of the 2010 Super Bowl, CBS television aired an ad featuring Heisman Trophy winner Tim Tebow and his mother, Pam. In a friendly, informal conversation they talked about her decision to give life (not to have an abortion). Pam's decision resulted in the birth of Tim Tebow—the same Tim Tebow who is now a starting quarterback in the National Football League.

> Suffering may also include ridicule from an immoral society.

The announcement of the planned TV ad created a firestorm of protest and liberal media hype. News commentator Susan Estrich called the ad run by Focus on the Family "deceptive and ultimately cruel."[3] Newspaper columnist and blogger John Romano denounced quarterback Tebow for the ad: "If he wants to align himself with a rather dogmatic organization such as Focus on the Family, that is his right. Just so long as he understands that intolerance, even when wrapped in religion, is still intolerance." Terry O'Neill, president of the National Organization of Women, called the ad, "extraordinarily offensive and demeaning."[4]

Strange. Encouraging mothers to give life to their babies rather than aborting them is called "intolerance." Proponents of a secular, humanist culture are tolerant as long as others don't conflict with their secular, amoral views. So suffering may also include ridicule from an immoral society.

OPPOSITION TO THE CHRISTIAN MESSAGE

From the inception of the gospel era, believers have suffered for the sake of the gospel. Sometimes the suffering came simply as a result of sacrifice and hardship for the sake of the gospel. At other times, because of hatred of Christ and the Christian message, believers have suffered simply because they have committed themselves to declaring the good news of Jesus Christ. And they stand in a long line of heroes of the faith.

The Book of Acts is rife with examples of God's servants who suffered for the gospel. As the apostles spread the gospel message in Jerusalem, Peter and John were arrested, imprisoned, and then put on trial and interrogated by the Sanhedrin (Acts 4:3–12). They were ridiculed publicly. As the Sanhedrin demanded to know how they had healed the lame man, they derided the apostles. They asked them, "By what power, or in what name, have you ["fellows like you," a term of derision] done this?" (Acts 4:7). But Peter presented the gospel to the Jewish leaders. And when Peter and John were warned not to speak of Jesus again, they courageously responded that their obligation was to obey God rather than men (Acts 4:19–20).

They continued to proclaim the gospel despite being threatened (Acts 4:21). Why? Because believers have a biblical mandate to announce the good news of salvation through Jesus Christ. God has given us the ministry of reconciliation, to tell the world that through Christ, God has reconciled people to Himself (2 Cor. 5:18–20). We are to urge those around us to respond to the offer of the gospel. That is the reason believers stand up for the gospel—even to the ultimate sacrifice.

When Paul showed his determination to go to Jerusalem, whatever the cost, the people recognized it was the Lord's will and agreed, "The will of the Lord be done!" (Acts 21:14). It may be the Lord's will that His chosen servant will suffer and even die for the gospel. The glory of knowing Christ and having the privilege of spreading the good news of the gospel far outweighs any earthly calamities that may come to a believer. There was nothing on this earth that could dissuade Paul from proclaiming Christ. He did not fear the repercussions, the sufferings, that could arise from the ministry. Through the centuries many faithful believers have echoed Paul's persistence in proclaiming the gospel, even to the point of death. Jim Elliot's words ring true today: "He is no fool who gives what he cannot keep to gain that which he cannot lose."

WHY SICKNESS AS WE SERVE?

Many who serve the Lord, whether in home or overseas mission service, have cut their terms short when sickness forced them to leave prematurely. Whether due to malaria, debilitating dysentery, or an accident on the field, missionaries have often had to leave a developing work early. Others begin a domestic mission only to stay one term and then leave. Jeff, a tender, committed Christian, desired to serve the Lord in full-time Christian ministry. He had lived in the South his entire life and was culturally southern in thought and practice. Jeff attended seminary and eventually applied to serve the Lord in home missions. With a burden for small communities, Jeff eventually was placed in a rural community in New York state. His challenge was to revive a dying church.

Jeff accepted the challenge and began his ministry in New York with great enthusiasm. But the cultural change was more than his tender personality could accept. He was eventually hospitalized with a nervous breakdown and ultimately returned to his rural home in the south.

Why does God allow Jeff and others who begin to serve Him

stateside or in another country to suffer? Jeff had left his comfortable, native surroundings to serve the Lord in a very unfamiliar culture. He did not understand the blunt approach of the people in his church and community. His sensitive nature crumbled under the direct approach of the northern people.

WHY WAS EPAPHRODITUS SICK?

Even in the early church, at times those who served Christ suffered sickness for the sake of the gospel. Epaphroditus, Paul's fellow worker, "was sick to the point of death" because of his work in the ministry (Phil. 2:27). Epaphroditus, who was probably a native of Philippi, carried Paul's epistle to the church at Philippi. Paul spoke highly of him. He was Paul's "fellow worker"; he had labored together with Paul in the gospel. He was also a fellow soldier, suggesting the spiritual warfare that he was engaged in with Paul, fighting the enemy side by side with Paul (Phil. 2:25; cf. Eph. 6:12). Epaphroditus was a messenger (*apostolon*), "a messenger sent on a special commission."[5] He was also Paul's minister (*leitourgon*), a term originally used to describe civil servants and later the priests who offered sacrifices in the temple.

Epaphroditus risked his own life and health for a spiritual ministry to Paul while the apostle was in prison. He was a humble servant of the Lord who was not concerned for his own welfare but rather the welfare of others. He had the heart of Christ in his love for the Philippian believers. Indeed, despite his own sickness, his concern was for them—he became distressed when he learned they "had heard that he was sick" (2:26). He was willing to serve others to the point that he became sick and was near death.

In the ministry Epaphroditus risked his life for the sake of the gospel (v. 30). Paul uses a colorful word to describe Epaphroditus's selflessness. "Risking" (*paraboleusamenos*) means "to play the gambler, to expose one's self to danger. The word has connotations of gambling or playing dice by which high sums were often at stake."[6]

Part of the answer to why there is sickness among those in service may be to become more Christlike. When a believer suffers physically to the point of sickness in service for Christ, his humility and selflessness is a picture of Christ Himself. In the same chapter, Paul reflected on the ultimate example of humility: Jesus Christ. The Lord Himself, who existed in the form of God, humbled Himself by taking on the form of a servant. He even became "obedient to the point of death on a cross" (Phil. 2:6–8).

TO SUFFER IS A PRIVILEGE

With this example, Paul exhorted the believers to "have this attitude in yourselves which was also in Christ Jesus" (v. 5). He also instructs them, "Do not merely look out for your own personal interests, but also for the interests of others" (v. 4). This may well involve suffering. Indeed, we are *called* to suffer. Paul reminds the Philippians: "For to you it has been granted for Christ's sake, not only to believe in Him, but also to suffer for His sake" (Phil. 1:29). "To suffer" is emphatic in the Greek text. We are called to this. Moreover, we have been "granted" this, meaning this is a "gift of grace" to suffer for Christ. To believe in Christ is a privilege; to suffer for Christ is a privilege.

One reason suffering is a privilege is because through suffering we come to know Christ. Paul stated, "That I may know Him and the power of His resurrection and the fellowship of His sufferings, being conformed to His death" (Phil. 3:10). "The fellowship of His sufferings . . ." It seems Paul was anticipating his death in this statement—suffering as his Savior suffered—giving up his life for the sake of the gospel. And it still happens.

PUTTING OTHERS FIRST

In a society that loudly proclaims, "Me first," the Scriptures teach, "Others first." We are to be other-centered. We are to focus on the needs of our neighbors. In expending ourselves for others, we sometimes will face inconvenience and even illness—and in extreme cases, death.

Timothy, Paul's son in the faith, seems to have been exactingly scrupulous in attempting to avoid offense, and as a result he became sick. Because water was often impure in New Testament times, believers used wine for medicinal purposes to alleviate illness from drinking impure water. Yet, to avoid offense, Timothy resisted drinking wine so that he would not be considered addicted to wine (cf. 1 Tim. 3:2). Paul instructed Timothy to drink wine as a medicinal help to cure his stomach ailments that resulted from the impure water (1 Tim. 5:23). Timothy had voluntarily suffered physically not to offend others, so there would be no offense in proclaiming the gospel.

"THAT . . . THE POWER MAY BE OF GOD"

Serving Christ may bring sickness and suffering. Christians possess bodies that succumb to sickness and disease like those of everyone else. Paul reminds us, "We have this treasure in earthen vessels" (2 Cor. 4:7). Paul is referring to clay pottery, capable of being broken and shattered. Specifically, "Paul may have been referring to the small pottery lamps which were cheap and fragile, or he may have referred to earthenware vases or urns. The point seems to be that the valuable treasure is contained in weak, fragile, and valueless containers."[7]

The reason we have this treasure of the gospel message in these bodies, that are subject to destruction, is "that the surpassing greatness of *the power may be of God and not from ourselves*" (2 Cor. 4:7, italics added). When we serve the Lord in responsibilities beyond ourselves, in stress that consumes us, in situations that frighten us, then God must extend His grace if we are to perform the ministry. Hence, Paul explains that "we are afflicted in every way, but not crushed; perplexed, but not despairing; persecuted, but not forsaken; struck down, but not destroyed; always carrying about in the body the dying of Jesus, that the life of Jesus also may be manifested in our body" (v. 8–10).

Notice Paul's terminology in describing the ministry: "afflicted . . . perplexed . . . persecuted . . . struck down." He is describing the hardship and suffering involved in ministry. Sickness and suffering come for many reasons, but here, the chief reason is the mortality of the human body. Our bodies are capable of suffering, and in the ministry there is suffering. But the suffering extols the power of God at work in us. That is Paul's point.

> Suffering extols the power of God at work in us.

In our suffering for the gospel we identify with Christ (v. 10). He suffered so that He might reveal the Father to a fallen humanity. Jesus suffered physically; He had no place to lay His head. He walked through Samaria so that He might give a despised people the good news. Weary and hungry He sat by the well of Sychar and gave the gospel to a needy woman (John 4:6 ff.). He suffered physically in bringing the gospel to the Samaritans. We identify with Christ when we accept hardship and suffering in bringing the gospel to spiritually needy people.

WILLIAM CAREY: A CASE STUDY IN PATIENT SUFFERING

William Carey reflects the heart of Christ in patient suffering for the sake of the gospel.[8] Burdened about the lost who had never heard the gospel, Carey, a native of England, sailed for India in 1793. Once on the mission field, he would suffer as few have suffered for the gospel. His first wife never shared his aspirations or ideals, yet Carey never complained. Fever and dysentery infected her so that her last twelve years were spent in madness before she died.

The following year, while serving in Serampore, Carey married Lady Rumohr, who shared both his intellect and his love for ministry to the Indian people. But his precious wife died after thirteen years of marriage.

On June 24, 1809, William Carey completed the Bengali translation of the entire Bible. Ultimately, Carey and his associates published the New Testament or the Bible in more than forty languages. But on March 11, 1812, Carey was away in Calcutta, and the native workers had gone from the building where the translation work was continuing. Suddenly, fire broke out in the building. Carey arrived the next day to view the devastation. Destroyed were his manuscripts, the Sikh and Telugoo grammars, ten Bible versions in the press, as well as other works. The translation of the Ramayana, which Carey and an associate had been developing, was stopped forever. Met with this devastating scene, Carey and his associates read Psalm 46—and immediately Carey took up the laborious translation work once more. His motto, "Expect great things from God; attempt great things for God," continued to be practiced.

Carey said of the devastating fire, "The loss is very great, and will long be severely felt; yet I can think of a hundred circumstances which would have made it much more difficult to bear. The Lord has smitten us, he had a right to do so, and we deserve his corrections. I wish to submit to His sovereign will, nay, cordially to acquiesce therein, and to examine myself rigidly to see what in me has contributed to this evil." Amid this horrific suffering and devastation, William Carey knew God is good and found peace.

GOOD OUT OF BAD

Eventually God would let Carey see the good He had in this suffering and loss. As a result of the fire, these translators and their work became famous, not only in India, but all over Europe and America. Christian educators and even secular people became interested in their work. Donations for their work poured in. In less than two months their financial loss was covered through donations raised in England and Scotland. And the translation work continued more effectively than ever.

Of the translations and grammars, Carey and his colleagues wrote: "We found, on making the trial, that the advantages in going over the same ground a second time were so great that they fully counter-balanced the time requisite to be devoted thereto in a second translation." In effect, the fire gave birth to revised editions. There was a reason for the fire and destruction—and William Carey recognized it.

WHO CAN FATHOM GOD'S WAYS?

Carey got an answer to his why, even though he did not request it. But it should be clear in this chapter that many times we will not learn why while on earth. Sometimes we can see the reasons; many times we cannot. But God is sovereign and wise and good; His ways are perfect whether we understand them or not. Although God unveiled the mystery of the fire that destroyed Carey's work, he never would learn why he buried two wives as well as other family members. In a distant nation and a radically different culture, he suffered hardship in his work. But while Carey suffered a great deal, he left a larger legacy through his ministry to the people of India. Through his translations, the gospel was read by millions of Indian people. Who can evaluate the suffering of a servant of God but, through that suffering, untold millions would now hear the gospel?

THE CALL TO SUFFERING

Suffering for the gospel is a common concept in Paul's letters to his young son in the faith. He exhorts Timothy to "join with me in suffering for the gospel" (2 Tim. 1:8) and "suffer hardship with me, as a good soldier of Christ Jesus" (2 Tim. 2:3). Paul reminds Timothy that he has followed his "teaching, conduct, purpose, faith, patience, love, perseverance, persecutions, and sufferings . . ." (2 Tim. 3:10–11). Paul explains that he suffers "hardship even to imprisonment as a criminal" (2 Tim. 2:9).

Paul reminds Timothy that serving Christ will involve hardship. He commissions Timothy to pass on the truth to trustworthy men who will likewise pass the baton of truth to others (2 Tim. 2:2). But in that process there will be hardship. Timothy needs to be self-disciplined like a soldier, faithful in battle, loyal to the one who has appointed him (v. 3). A soldier has a singular purpose—to win the war.

The soldier is not diverted from his primary task. He cannot afford to be wrapped up in secondary matters. Paul instructs Timothy, "No soldier in active service entangles himself in the affairs of everyday life, so that he may please the one who enlisted him as a soldier" (v. 4). In suffering hardship so that the gospel of Christ will prosper, the servant of Jesus Christ will live by a singular focus. On doubtful things and on secondary things he will live by the maxim, "Others may; I cannot." And so he suffers hardship. It may mean separation from loved ones because the work of the gospel takes him to foreign countries; it may mean financial hardship through willingly giving up opportunities for financial prosperity in order to serve Christ. It may mean expending oneself in service for Christ, giving up an easy life. It may mean suffering physically by extending oneself in ministry. Today Christ calls His own to suffer hardship with Him, just as Paul called Timothy.

THE MESSAGE

The apostle Paul willingly risked his life for the glorious gospel: "Remember Jesus Christ, risen from the dead" (2 Tim. 2:8). This was the message that motivated Paul. The shackles of sin and the doom of death was broken in the bodily resurrection of Christ! When Jesus came out of the tomb, He freed humanity from despair and hopelessness.

The resurrection was the message "for which I suffer hardship even to imprisonment as a criminal; but the word of God is not imprisoned" (2 Tim. 2:9). Paul gladly suffered imprisonment and hardship for the sake of the gospel. What a profound message Paul could convey! Jesus Christ "abolished death and brought life and immortality to light through the gospel" (1:10). Weighed in the light of eternity, the suffering of the servant of God is inconsequential when compared with the glories and joy of heaven.

THE MAIN REASON TO SUFFER FOR THE GOSPEL

Why suffer for the gospel? The main reason is the nature of the glorious gospel itself. The gospel of Jesus Christ saves people from eternal destruction and brings them into eternal joy and bliss. The gospel is worth the cost. The gospel of Jesus Christ that sets men and women free from slavery to Satan and death is worth the suffering.

When Paul met with the elders of Ephesus, he reminded them that both prisoner's chains and suffering awaited him in Jerusalem (Acts 20:23). What was Paul's response? "I do not consider my life of any account as dear to myself, so that I may finish my course and the ministry which I received" (v. 24).

As Paul faced possible execution by the Roman authorities, he evaluated his life. Was the suffering worth it? Was his life of hardship and his premature death worth it? Paul concluded, "I have fought the good fight, I have finished the course, I have kept the faith; in the future there is laid up for me the crown of righteousness, which the Lord, the righteous Judge, will award to me on that day; and not only to me, but also to all who have loved His appearing" (2 Tim. 4:7–8).

To Paul the gospel was a good and noble cause. The apostle had faithfully maintained the precious gospel that had been entrusted to him. No wreath of victory, no trophy awarded an athlete at the Olympic Games could ever compare with the award

Paul—and believers who would follow in his train—would receive. At Christ's return, Paul would receive a crown of righteousness. It would be his reward for faithful service.[9] That was Paul's prospect, and that is the prospect of all who serve the Lord faithfully in this brief life.

Why suffer for the gospel? God's people view the gospel as a precious treasure entrusted to their safekeeping. Believers willingly take their stand for the truth of the gospel. It is an imperative, but it is also a privilege. Succeeding generations depend on the faithfulness of God's people today. The purity of the gospel tomorrow can only be measured by the faithfulness of God's people in standing firm for its truth today.

Suffering may come to Christians who defend the gospel. There may be physical suffering through deprived living conditions on foreign soil, or it may involve rejection and ridicule in the western world. But the eternal gospel of Jesus Christ is worthy of us expending ourselves for its truth. And on that future day, when the Lord, the Righteous Judge, awards His faithful servants, the questions we have today will be resolved.

9

What's the Purpose of Suffering?

In our sufferings, peace can occur only when we reflect on the enormity of the divine transaction that occurred when Christ died on our behalf. Theologians refer to our righteous standing through Christ as our *justification* before God

The apostle Paul puts it this way: "Therefore, having been justified by faith, we have peace with God through our Lord Jesus Christ" (Rom. 5:1). Who can fathom the divine declaration of grace in our being judged righteous in Christ? Out of His bountiful grace, God accomplished for us what we could never achieve ourselves. He fitted us for heaven, and all through His grace.

As a result, Paul says, "We exult in hope of the glory of God" (v. 2). This is strong language. It means that we rejoice, we boast, we triumphantly rejoice in our confident position in Christ.[1] Why? Because, writes Bible commentator C. K. Barrett, we have a "rejoicing confidence . . . in God. The man who has been justified exults in good hope for the future, knowing that he can look forward to nothing less than the glory of God."[2]

Paul transitions in his letter when he writes, "And not only this, but we also exult in our tribulations" (v. 3). We would wish that Paul had stopped in verse 2, but he didn't. He uses the same strong language. Paul says believers triumphantly boast in their tribulations.

Suffering does not stifle the believer's confident joy in his position in Christ. Far from it. Suffering itself becomes an avenue of rejoicing confidence in Christ because, if allowed to fulfill its purpose, suffering will lead to greater maturity.

A PURPOSE OF PERSEVERANCE

When our son, Jeremy, then sixteen, tore a ligament in his arm just when the baseball season was beginning, we didn't tell him to thank God for his torn ligament. We encouraged him; we expressed our regret that he wouldn't be playing baseball for a while. Some folks confuse this issue. When a man broke his leg he said, "I thanked God for my broken leg." That really is not the intention of Romans 5:3.

The Christian who has been diagnosed with terminal cancer does not thank God *for* the cancer. Paul emphasizes that we triumph *in* our tribulations, but we don't thank God *for* our tribulations. There is a difference.[3]

For the believer, suffering has a divine purpose. If we allow tribulation to realize its purpose in our lives, it will produce perseverance. This is a unique word in the original Greek (*hupomone*); it means "to remain under." When people say, "Oh, I'm all right— under the circumstances," some respond in jest, "What are you doing under the circumstances? You should be living above the circumstances!" It is a humorous response—but not quite accurate. "Perseverance" (*hupomone*) means "patient endurance, patiently waiting in hope."[4] In hope, the suffering believer bears up patiently amid the trials that have come upon him. He sees the sovereign hand of God at work—for good—in leading him through the dark valleys. But the valleys produce maturity in perseverance.

PITCHING IN THE BIG LEAGUES

Dave Dravecky had a childhood dream of playing major league baseball.[5] His dream came true when he entered the majors in 1982 and pitched in the All-Star game the following year. In October 1984, through the playoffs and world series, Dave pitched in relief five times, a total of 10-2/3 innings. He did not allow one run to score.

But Dave's elbow and shoulder pain plagued him. A trade to the Giants allowed him some time of rest. In the National League Championship series on July 4, 1987 Dave posted a 5–0 playoff shutout over the Cardinals in Game 2 and extended his scoreless postseason to 19-2/3 innings. He gave up only one run in Game 6. When Dave discovered a lump on his throwing arm, he remained unconcerned.

He began the Giants' 1988 season pitching at Dodger Stadium. On the first pitch, Dravecky gave up a home run. "Then Dave 'locked in,' shut down the Dodgers on three hits, and won 5 to 1. Returning home, he told his wife, Janice, 'I think 1988 is going to be my year!'"

THE RIGHT RESPONSE

But the season didn't turn out the way Dave anticipated. Manager Roger Craig pulled Dave from the rotation because of his troubling shoulder. Arthroscopic surgery was necessary to repair torn tendons in his shoulder. Dave did not pitch again that year. Following a disappointing season, Dave had the lump on his arm diagnosed: a malignant tumor.

Thinking about his wife and two children—and his own eternal destiny, Dave was overwhelmed by a deep sense of security. That peace had begun seven years earlier, when Byron Ballard, a teammate, had shared the gospel with him, and both Dave and Janice trusted in Jesus Christ as their personal Savior. "It transformed our response to the news we heard seven years later. It prevented us from responding to the tumor with bitterness and anger, because the God who revealed Himself through Jesus is full of love. That gave us a deep well of hope to draw on."

In the fall of 1988, the surgeon removed the tumor and surrounding muscle tissue, cutting away half the deltoid of the left shoulder and upper arm, destroying 95 percent of that muscle's function. The surgeon told Janice, "He will never pitch again."

But Dave was determined and began therapy . . . agonizing therapy. He progressed to full-scale workouts, and Dave pitched in the minors in 1989. On August 10, 1989, he returned to the Giants, and pitching against the Cardinals, posted a significant eight-inning, 4 to 3 performance. And publicly Dave gave God all the credit.

The next week, Dave pitched in Montreal, and "during a sixth-inning delivery to the Expos' Tim Raines, Dave's arm snapped with such ferocity that the crack was heard all over the field." Weeks later he joined teammates on the baseball diamond to celebrate the Giants clinching the National League championship, but his mending arm broke again during the players' on-field celebration. After the season was over, he discovered the tumor had returned. The injury and reappearance of the tumor ended Dravecky's career.

"I had to learn to do what was within my grasp, and leave control of the rest to God."

When reporters asked whether the year of painful, uncertain rehabiliation was worth it to pitch just two more games in the majors, Dave answered, "Yes, it was worth it, a million times over. It was worth it on another level, too, because of the growth it brought in my life. I had to learn to do what was within my grasp, one day at a time, and leave control of the rest to God."[6]

Why did Dave Dravecky develop the malignant tumor on his throwing arm? Why did his brilliant career in the major leagues have to end? In this story as in other stories, the complete answer remains with an all-wise, sovereign God. However, Dave himself explained the reason as he saw it. It produced growth in his Christian life; it enabled him to make a genuine, spiritual "comeback." That is true for all who experience adversity. It enables them to experience the most significant comeback of all—growth and perseverance through Christ. Dave recognized everything happens for a reason, and he exhibited courageous endurance.

In Chapter 7 we repeatedly asked the question "Why?" We saw that during persecution, believers can (1) bring honor to Christ, (2) realize Satan is at work, trying to undermine our faith, (3) develop and demonstrate faith in God, and (4) demonstrate joy. Baseball pitcher Dave Dravecky also shows that suffering can also bring growth and perseverance.

In the early church, amid much persecution and suffering, the Thessalonian believers also learned about the value of perseverance, so much so that the apostle Paul spoke of their courageous endurance to other churches (2 Thess. 1:4).

When Paul brought the gospel to Thessalonica, opposition arose. Critics of the gospel became jealous and recruited evil men, forming a mob against Paul and the nucleus of new believers (Acts 17:1–9). They were dragged before the city authorities and charged with criminal activity. Yet amid all the opposition and persecution, the Thessalonian believers persevered, and their faith and love grew greater (1 Thess. 1:3–4). Undoubtedly, the Thessalonians could see the imprint of God's hand in all these events.

James conveys a similar message. James also reminds believers that "the testing of your faith produces endurance" (James 1:3). The believer's testing (*peirasmois*) is for the purpose of revealing the genuineness or good quality of the person. The testing is not intended for failure but for triumph, for victory. It is like the gold mineral that is subjected to the heat of the smelter's fire. The singular purpose is to show the good quality of the gold. That is the purpose in the believer's testing through suffering—to bring the believer forth as gold tried by fire.

PRODUCING SPIRITUAL MATURITY

James was addressing Jewish believers who were part of the Diaspora, the dispersion of Jews among the Gentile nations (1:1). They were likely suffering persecution for two reasons: because they were Jews and because they were believers in Jesus Christ. Moreover, the opposition against these Jewish Christians was not isolated—they were encountering "various trials" (v. 2). James admonished them to endure, to remain steadfast amid the trials. Resistance to the trials would make the trials ineffective. But by remaining steadfast, persevering amid the trials, the final purpose of the trials would be achieved—spiritual maturity (v. 4).

Unquestionably, we fail to understand many of the things that happen to us. Why this illness? Why the family tragedies? Why this loneliness? What is the reason? When there is a lack of understanding, James exhorts us to pray for wisdom (v. 5).

Although we do not have answers to each of those questions, and we often will pray for wisdom, we do know the final purpose is our spiritual maturity. Thus Dave Dravecky could say the pain "was worth it. . . because of the [spiritual] growth it brought" in his life.

Repeatedly in the Scriptures we are reminded of the value of suffering and the spiritual lessons we learn. Further, through the sufferings we see the faithfulness of God. Psalm 94:12–14 declares, "Blessed is the man whom You chasten, O Lord, and whom You teach out of Your law; that you may grant him relief from the days of adversity, until a pit is dug for the wicked. For the Lord will not abandon His people, nor will He forsake His inheritance." The psalmist reminds us that the Lord will rescue us and grant us relief in our adversity. If others have afflicted us, there will be divine retribution on them. But the overriding truth is clear: "The Lord will not abandon His people."

This is a significant lesson for us. While we wait for the Lord to deliver us from our trials, we must remain rooted in His Word, finding consolation and peace in the Scriptures. There is a reason and purpose in our suffering.

ANOTHER BASEBALL STORY

I've told the story of two injuries on the athletic field. Here's one more story about the baseball diamond and my son Jeremy. Now a thirty-one-year-old father, Jeremy and his wife, Kim, were excitedly looking forward to the birth of their second child. Jeremy hadn't lost his love of baseball, though, and had joined the church softball team. During the last game of the year, Jeremy hit the ball in what appeared to be an in-the-park home run. As he rounded second base, he heard a "pop." He thought the second base bag had hit his leg. But when he took one more step, he realized what had happened. An unscheduled trip to the emergency room at the hospital revealed that he had torn the Achilles tendon completely off the bone.

The surgeon had never seen an injury of that nature. After a complex surgery, months of painful therapy awaited Jeremy. The physician would need to recast his foot four times; each time he moved the foot to a new, painful position.

The ensuing weeks brought considerable pain, both physically and emotionally for the family. Unable to walk, Jeremy was entirely housebound and totally dependent on his wife and others—and Kim was nearly nine months pregnant.

Kim had experienced several difficulties during her pregnancy. This led to several additional visits to the obstetrician for tests and exams. Although everything turned out well, the situation caused considerable stress. The baby had also moved to a position that put extreme pressure on a nerve in Kim's back. Now, near the end of her pregnancy, Kim was moving slowly and unable to carry Jacob, their one-year-old boy. And Jeremy could help her little.

One month after Jeremy's surgery, Kim went into labor during the night, two weeks prior to the physician's scheduled induction of labor. But Jeremy was unable to drive his wife to the hospital. He had previously made arrangements for the neighbor to take her to the hospital, but when he called his neighbor that night, he discovered his neighbor was on vacation. Finally, a friend who was housesitting for the neighbor took Kim to the hospital.

God blessed Jeremy and Kim with Joel, a beautiful, healthy baby boy. Within two days Kim and the baby were home. But Jeremy was still relegated to sitting in a chair most of the day. Kim was recovering from the birth of a child; an infant was present with numerous needs, and their one-and-a-half-year-old son, Jacob, was busily running throughout the house.

There sat Jeremy, as months of painful therapy and four different casts awaited. Those months would be difficult; yet, by the grace of God, Jeremy and Kim persevered. Through the difficulties they experienced growth in their relationship with the Lord. Jeremy explains: "Although trials are never enjoyable at the time, they certainly help in forming the character God wants us to have. As individuals who strive to have organized, planned-out days, our summer created a challenge for us. It led us to give up control and to tell God that only He could get us through our situation. It was so overwhelming we felt numb and powerless. We knew only God could carry us

> "We felt numb and powerless. We knew only God could carry us through."

through (1 Pet. 5:7). During this time we spent more time in prayer than ever before."

CHARACTER DEVELOPMENT:
MOVING TOWARD SPIRITUAL MATURITY

For Jeremy and Kim, the pain brought spiritual growth toward maturity, or as Jeremy puts it, the "forming [of] the character God wants us to have." Along the way, fellow believers expressed love and support through cards, letters, and prayers. "It helped to know that there were so many people lifting us up before God. Many people from church brought us meals to help us—even people with whom we had little or no previous relationship."

God uses others to help sustain us during suffering. Jeremy and Kim felt the blessing of God through so many friends who came to their assistance.

In Romans 5, Paul teaches that perseverance produces proven character (Rom. 5:4). On their way to proven character and greater spiritual maturity, Jeremy and Kim underwent the trials of an immobilizing foot cast and a complicated pregnancy. Significantly, "proven character" (*dokimen*) in verse 4 denotes "the quality of being approved as result of tests and trials."[7] As Alan Johnson wrote in his classic study of Romans, "Our persevering attitude in trials brings glory to Him and thus a tried, or proven, character to us (2 Cor. 11:30; 12:9). When we are brought to the place where we have nothing else but God, we suddenly realize He is all we need."[8]

James 1:2–4 has a similar emphasis. James tells believers to rejoice in tribulations because in them God can do His refining work on the believer. For Jeremy and Kim, this was God's divine chisel in action.

THE OUTCOME OF PROVEN CHARACTER: HOPE

When proven character arrives, it issues in hope. This hope is fixed on the glory of God—the glorious manifestation of God at the triumphant return of Christ. Paul began with hope, and he concludes with hope (Rom. 5:2, 4–5). This hope is a strong confidence in God. We may say, "I hope it won't rain this weekend." That is merely expressing a wish, but it does not exhibit a confidence. Biblical hope is confidence. Hope (*elpis*) is an "expectation . . . hope in God's promises."[9]

Though experiencing trials, the believer who rests his hope in God will not be disappointed because God's love for him will flood his heart (Rom. 5:5–8). He will press on amid the difficult issues of life, knowing that his confident hope in the Lord is valid.

A MUSLIM IN HOUSTON

Although he was born in Houston, Texas, Afshin Ziafat returned to his native country of Iran when he was only two. But his father, a medical doctor and devout Muslim, faced a serious decision when the Iranian people, led by the Muslim clerics, overthrew the Shah. The new Islamic leaders would decide who would practice medicine. Determined to practice medicine unhindered, the father and his family returned to Houston.[10]

When Afshin was in the second grade, his Christian public school teacher gave him a New Testament with the advice: "You are too young to read this now, but someday I want you to read this." When Afshin arrived home, he threw the New Testament in a closet. The New Testament remained in the closet, unread, for ten years.

As a high school senior, Afshin was provoked to investigate the claims of Christianity through a television show. Remembering the New Testament, he found it and began to read it. He read Matthew in one sitting. The account of Christ's life moved him. When Afshin read Romans, the Holy Spirit opened his heart and he trusted in Jesus Christ as his Savior.

TRUSTING THE SAVIOR, FEARING THE FAMILY

He began to listen to Christian radio and secretly attend church services. Fearing his father would discover Afshin's newfound faith, he hid the New Testament in the bottom of a drawer, along with other Christian materials. Afshin discreetly intercepted Christian literature that was being sent to him so his family wouldn't find out. He hid his Sunday clothes in his car on Saturday evening and changed clothes in a restaurant on Sunday morning before going to church so his father wouldn't discover where he was going.

Following high school graduation, Afshin went off to the University of Texas, pursuing medical studies like his father. Those in the church Afshin had been attending prayed that Afshin would get a Christian roommate who would be an encouragement to him. In the providence of God, Afshin discovered he had a Christian roommate at college—a converted former Muslim! God had answered prayer. It was God's grace and sovereignty in looking after Afshin when he was hurting after being ostracized from his family. The young men encouraged each other in their faith.

One weekend when Afshin returned home, his father confronted him. He had discovered the truth. When he told his father he was a Christian, his father tersely reminded him, "You are a Muslim. You will always be a Muslim."

THE COST OF FOLLOWING CHRIST

Afshin remained adamant in his faith in Christ. "If you want to be a Christian, you can no longer be my son," Afshin's father told him. Afshin struggled—he even thought of abandoning his faith in Christ. But he couldn't. "Dad, if I had to choose between you and Jesus, I would choose my heavenly Father." His father told him he had two weeks to gather his things and get out of the house.

Broken and fearful, Afshin left home, returning to the University of Texas and crying out to God for help. Then Afshin read the shocking words of Matthew 10:32, 37–38: "Everyone who confesses Me before men, I will also confess him before My father who is in heaven. . . . He who loves father or mother more than Me is not worthy of Me. And he who does not take his cross and follow after Me is not worthy of Me."

Later a miracle occurred. After a year of separation from his home, his father invited him to come back. They were reconciled. Afshin's father accepted him back.

But as Afshin was growing in his faith, he was confronted with another crisis: What would he do with his life? He had been studying pre-med, intending to follow his father in medicine. But the Holy Spirit was working, and at the crisis Afshin surrendered to the gospel ministry. Yet this meant another crisis in his home. What would his father say?

The day came when Afshin divulged his commitment to the Christian ministry. In Afshin's own words, "It broke my father's heart. He told me it was the biggest blemish on his life . . . that I had died in his heart. I have the greatest father in the world, one who has devoted his life to his family. But he had to stand by his strong Muslim convictions."

Afshin followed through with his Christian convictions and has pursued the gospel ministry. Although the relationship has been strained, God is at work. Afshin's sister also became a Christian, and more recently Afshin's father accepted a Bible and promised to read it.

THE PAIN OF REJECTION

Afshin Ziafat has discovered the cost of being a Christian. Being rejected by his father and told that he was "the biggest blemish on his life," Afshin has truly counted the cost of following Christ. He has discovered the words of Christ, "Do not think that I came to bring peace on the earth; I did not come to bring peace, but a sword. For I came to set a man against his father . . . a man's enemies will be the members of his household . . . He who has found his life shall lose it, and he who has lost his life for My sake shall find it" (Matt. 10:34–36, 39).

When a person becomes a believer in Jesus Christ, bad things may come at the hands of those the believer loves the most, his or her family members. Afshin is not the first, nor will he be the last person to be rejected by family members because he became a Christian. Frequently those of other faiths roundly reject the family member who has come to faith in Christ. Jesus predicted this would happen.

Countless believers have experienced rejection and ostracism because they identify with Christ.

There is a cost to following Christ. Countless believers have experienced rejection, suffering, and ostracism because of their identification with Christ. They have been passed over in job promotions. They have been sent away from home. A young boy was thrown out of his home, left to fend for himself in the streets of Tampa, because his atheistic father didn't want a Christian son.

But Christ reminds us that only as we take up the cross and follow Him, are we worthy of Him. It is only as we lose our lives for Christ that we truly find our lives.

RESPONDING TO REJECTION AND RIDICULE

Setting himself as a model of one subjected to ridicule, Paul wisely warned us how we are to think when we suffer for Christ through ridicule and rejection. Calling the apostles seemingly "fools for Christ's sake" (1 Cor. 4:10), he described their situation and their response: "To this present hour we are both hungry and thirsty, and are poorly clothed, and are roughly treated, and are homeless; and we toil, working with our own hands; when we are reviled, we bless; when we are persecuted, we endure; when we are slandered, we try to conciliate" (4:11–13).

Like the early apostles, we have to decide how we will respond. Will we become bitter . . . angry . . . vengeful? Trials can be a test. Do I have a high view of myself? Am I self-centered in my thinking? These inspired words of Scripture are instructive. I must gladly accept the indignations that come to me. With humility of heart I accept the appellation, "fool for Christ." Instead of revenge I must seek conciliation.

There is no need that exceeds God's supply of grace.

Suffering for Christ is an opportunity to grow spiritually through blessing those who are hostile, through enduring amid persecution, through being conciliatory when slandered. It is a test of our maturity.

Paul reiterated the thought in Romans 12:14, "Bless those who persecute you; bless and do not curse." He expanded on these words in Romans 12:17–21:

> *Never pay back evil for evil to anyone. Respect what is right in the sight of all men. If possible, so far as it depends on you, be at peace with all men. Never take your own revenge, beloved, but leave room for the wrath of God, for it is written, "Vengeance is Mine, I will repay," says the Lord. "But if your enemy is hungry, feed him, and if he is thirsty, give him a drink; for in so doing you will heap burning coals on his head." Do not be overcome by evil, but overcome evil with good.*

ABUNDANT GRACE

In our maturing process, God supplies sufficient grace for the moment. There is no need that exceeds God's supply of grace. It is always sufficient. When Paul prayed three times to the Lord concerning the thorn in his flesh, God answered his prayer—but differently from what Paul had requested. Rather than removing Paul's affliction, the Lord supplied grace. He reminded the apostle, "My grace is sufficient for you, for power is perfected in weakness" (2 Cor. 12:9). And Paul himself was able to conclude, "Most gladly, therefore, I will rather boast about my weaknesses, so that the power of Christ may dwell in me. Therefore I am well content with weaknesses, with insults, with distresses, with persecutions, with difficulties, for Christ's sake; for when I am weak, then I am strong" (vv. 9b–10).

Through God's grace, Paul could boast about his weaknesses (v. 9). Paul was content; he actually took pleasure in his weaknesses because it extolled the power of Christ in his life. Yet the list of Paul's sufferings is significant: weaknesses, public insults and humiliation, distresses, persecutions, and difficulties. But amid the troubles and trials, Christ infuses His strength, overshadowing our weaknesses.

John reminds us: "Of His fullness we have all received, and grace upon grace" (1:16). This valuable verse reminds us that the grace of God is inexhaustible. When we are in difficulty and need God's grace, He faithfully supplies it. But the next day we need more grace. He supplies it—"grace upon grace." We can never say, "I can't take it anymore." God's grace is abundant and will lift us up in our hour of need. When family and friends reject us, God's limitless grace is poured out, and we receive comfort and courage to go on.

The reason bad things may happen to us is to mature us. Along the way, his abundant grace will be ours, to bring us to a place of contentment. God's grace will always overshadow the bad things that happen to believers.

IT IS WELL WITH MY SOUL

When peace like a river, attendeth my way, when sorrows
    like sea billows roll;
Whatever my lot, Thou has taught me to say, It is well, it
    is well, with my soul.

One hundred fifty years ago, a man in grief wrote those majestic opening words to the classic hymn, "It Is Well with My Soul." Those words of peace and comfort continue to encourage and bless countless Christians. But these words were penned from a broken heart that defies description.

Horatio G. Spafford, a successful lawyer and investor, was also an active Christian, developing a close association with D. L. Moody and other Christian leaders. When the Great Chicago Fire occurred in 1871, it destroyed Spafford's real estate investments he had made only months earlier along the Lake Michigan shore. Shortly afterward, "his only son, age four, succumbed to scarlet fever. Horatio drowned his grief in work, pouring himself into rebuilding the city and assisting the 100,000 who had been left homeless."[11]

Two years later, he decided to take his wife and four daughters with him on a business trip to England. After the business portion, everyone would enjoy a vacation. At the last moment Spafford's business dealings prevented him from joining his family, so his wife and four daughters sailed without him. But on November 22, 1873, their ship, the S.S. *Ville du Havre*, was struck by an English vessel, the *Lochearn*, and their ship sank in only twelve minutes.

The survivors were taken to Cardiff, Wales, where Mrs. Spafford cabled her husband, "Saved Alone." Their four daughters had drowned in the shipwreck.

Horatio immediately booked passage to join his wife. En route, on a cold December night, the captain called him aside and said, "I believe we are now passing over the place where the *Ville du Havre* went down." Spafford went to his cabin but found it hard to sleep. He said to himself, "It is well; the will of God be done."

He later wrote his famous hymn based on those words. [12]

How will we respond to suffering and loss? Will we become bitter . . . angry . . . vengeful? Or will we seek God's abundant grace? Remember, there is no need that exceeds God's supply of grace. It is always sufficient.

10

How Our Loss Can
Benefit Others

Chris and Samantha Conti rejoiced as God gave them a beautiful daughter, their first child, Tia Grace. But the rejoicing was short-lived as the doctors explained that Tia Grace had serious problems. Because she was born at only thirty-one weeks gestation, she had underdeveloped vital organs. But even more seriously, Tia had what is known as transposition of the great arteries, a congenital heart defect.

Other complications existed. Tia Grace had extensive bleeding in her brain and some organs. Her prognosis of survival was 50/50, with only a 25 percent chance that she would be normal. Later, the doctors informed Chris and Samantha that Tia Grace was bleeding, which could result in mental retardation, cerebral palsy, or learning disabilities.

Christians prayed along with Chris and Samantha, and it appeared Tia Grace would recover. Doctors were calling her the "miracle baby," unable to explain why Tia Grace was responding and appeared to be gaining health.

Samantha prayed that Tia Grace might be healed but also

stated, "I do realize this may not be God's plan, and so I am also praying that God will prepare Chris and me for whatever road he chooses to take us down."[1]

Five weeks after her birth, the doctors operated on Tia to reconstruct her heart. The five-hour surgery was too much for Tia Grace. She died soon afterward.

A CHILD'S FUNERAL

Through all their heartache, Chris and Samantha exhibited enormous faith and trust in a sovereign God. At the funeral service Chris remarked, "We know that we have a good God, a God of comfort. But Deuteronomy 29:29 tells us that the secret things belong to the Lord our God. God has given us His Word and He has given us His Son. We are to love God and love one another. God isn't good because He gives us good things; He is good because He does good things. These are the lessons we have learned.

"We are blessed even though we will go through mourning," Chris continued. "God uses these times to draw us closer to Him. He never gives us more than we can bear. We can still have the joy of the Lord and a song in our hearts.

"We have learned so much about God's power in prayer. We have felt God's long arms wrapped around us. We have never doubted God's love in this. We need to look for God in every circumstance; that has helped us get through these trying days."

Chris and Samantha are great examples of God's grace in the midst of suffering. They are a profound encouragement to others who are suffering and a strong testimony of simple faith in God's sovereignty—without knowing "why."

FAITH AMID THE DARKNESS

After the death of Tia Grace, Chris and Samantha wrote their friends a letter, recounting their feelings and their spiritual journey:

We all have times of darkness in our lives. God uses these times to draw us closer to Him and refine us—if we allow Him. We have the choice to embrace the darkness with bitterness and resentment and learn nothing or to fall before the face of God relying on His strength to carry us through. We chose to accept the path God was taking us down, with teachable hearts, knowing He would never give us more than we could bear. We never thought we could ever handle losing a child. But God equipped us with all we have needed to not only survive this, but to keep the joy of the Lord and a song in our hearts.

It is important to look at what is right with the picture during the tough times—to look for God in every circumstance and try to see things from His perspective. When you choose to look for the good in any situation, you will be surprised at all the blessings to be found. That helped us get through each day and rejoice in even the smallest of things. We could have lost Tia the first couple of days, but instead we had 5½ glorious weeks with her. Although we lost Tia during heart surgery, we had three awesome days with her at duPont Hospital for Children that we otherwise would not have had. We got to room with her and be with her 24/7. For the first time since she was born, we actually felt like normal parents. We got to hold her whenever we wanted. We went to sleep and woke up with her right there with us.

They concluded their letter by mentioning one clear outcome from Tia's early homegoing: "God used His light within us to reach other families that we're hurting just as we were. . . . We believe God will continue to give us ministry opportunities to reach hurting families. The Bible says in 2 Corinthians 1:3–4, 'Blessed be the God and Father of our Lord Jesus Christ, the Father of mercies and God of all comfort, who comforts us in all our affliction so that we will be able to comfort those who are in any affliction with the comfort with which we ourselves are comforted by God.'"

Many encouraging and consoling letters poured into Chris and Samantha after Tia Grace's death, as others expressed their love and the effect of the Contis' trust in the Lord through their suffering. One, from Linda, told of her own strengthened faith during a similar loss.

"Your situation has so closely mirrored our own . . . Our little girl was born six weeks premature, after an eventful pregnancy," wrote Linda. "With each Dr. visit, we found more 'problems' . . . She lived almost four weeks in the hospital, touching countless lives during her own struggle.

> Their grief was intense, but their trust in God's sovereign work was just as intense.

"I never would have believed that a little one who never uttered a word could witness God's love to so many! But, as you have experienced, many are deeply touched by the life and death of a little child. Praise be to our sovereign God, who works these amazing things for His glory!"

Like Chris and Samantha, Linda could trust and praise the sovereign God, who is working all things for His glory. The witness of these parents impacts untold lives with the supernatural strength and peace that Jesus Christ alone can give.

Chris and Samantha had lost a child. Yet there was no confusion in their hearts. They saw the "bad thing" that was happening to them in the light of God's sovereignty. Although their sorrow and grief was intense over the death of their beloved child, their trust in God's sovereign work was just as intense. And it gave them a supernatural peace.

They did not see the death of their child as a result of a chaotic world of random happenings, a world that God Himself cannot control. Instead, their faith rested in the God of Scripture, the all-wise, sovereign God who makes no mistakes.

They recognized that God was ministering His comfort to them and through them to comfort others who were undergoing similar experiences. They have reached out to many other hurting people to minister to them. They have recognized the significance of 2 Corinthians 1:3-11 in their lives.

LOST CHILDREN . . . AND SUSTAINING FAITH

As tragic as the loss of one child, imagine those who endure the loss of several family members. On November 8, 1994, Scott Willis, a Chicago pastor, was driving home with his wife, Janet, and six of their nine children when the truck ahead of him dropped a piece of metal onto the expressway. Too late to change lanes, Pastor Willis had to let the object go under his vehicle. He hoped it would clear the van's undercarriage. Instead, it punctured the van's gas tank. Author Erwin Lutzer writes what happened next:

The rear gas tank exploded and five of the six Willis children died instantly in the flames. The sixth child, Benjamin, died a few hours later.

Scott and Janet were able to get out of the vehicle, sustaining burns from which they would later recover. Standing there watching their children die in the fire, Scott said to Janet, "This is the moment for which we are prepared." The courage of this couple was reported throughout the United States and the world. Christ walked with them through the deep sorrows of this tragedy.

"Every morning we awake we say, this is one more day to prove the faithfulness of God. Every night we say, we are one day closer to seeing our children again."[2]

SPIRITUAL BENEFIT FOR OTHERS

We can only imagine the pain Scott and Janet Willis experienced. Yet the death of these six children was not in vain. Eternity alone will tell of the spiritual impact this event made upon others as they recognized the spiritual endurance and stability of faith the Willis family exhibited. As Scott Willis faced a press conference, he quoted Psalm 34:1: "I will bless the Lord at all times; His praise shall continually be in my mouth." When reporters asked him "Why do bad things happen to good people?" he responded that "God had reasons . . . and that God was good."[3] Their faith in a sovereign God enabled Scott and Janet Willis to accept the early homegoing of their six children.

SUPERNATURAL COMFORT

In the first chapter of 2 Corinthians, the apostle Paul wrote to the church at Corinth about the sufferings he faced—afflictions he suffered and they suffered (see especially 2 Corinthians 4–7). As Paul contemplated the subject of suffering, he broke into a eulogy to the Lord: "Blessed be the God and Father of our Lord Jesus Christ" (v. 3). "Blessed" is the Greek word *eulogetos*. We get the English word "eulogize" from this— *eulogetos* means to speak well of someone. "Blessed" is a "Jewish ascription of praise to God acknowledging Him as the source of all blessing"[4] Do you get the picture? Paul praises God amid all the sufferings he has experienced and which he recounts in chapters 4 and 11.

Some people get bitter, even angry at God when they suffer. Not Paul. After his sufferings he could still praise God. He recognized that the things that happened to him were not an accident; they were ordained by God.

In the loss of a close family member, God offers His supernatural comfort. Amid the suffering and grief, God dispenses His mercy and comfort in abundance. The Scripture describes the heavenly Father as the "Father of mercies" and "God of all comfort" (1:3).

As the God of mercy, He has pity and compassion for His people. God doesn't "pass by on the other side" when we suffer. He extends mercy to us. James reminds us that "the Lord is full of compassion and is merciful" (James 5:11). This means God is "very kind, very pitiful, very sympathetic, [and] extremely compassionate."[5]

> Those who walk through the deep valleys of suffering experience the mountain peaks of God's great compassion.

We do not walk alone in our suffering! Only those who have walked through the deep valleys of suffering have experienced the mountain peaks of God's great compassion. And it is God's great compassion to us that enables us to endure.

God also extends His comfort to those who are suffering. "Comfort" (*parakleseos*) means "one called alongside to help." This word "Helper" is also a title of the Holy Spirit (John 14:16). God is an immanent God—He deigns to walk with us amid our suffering; He condescends to provide His presence in our trials.

SUPERNATURAL PEACE

Remember the response of Horatio Spafford? Amid the loss of his four daughters at sea, Spafford was nonetheless sustained by the peace of God. The words to "It Is Well With My Soul" came out of his great grief matched by supernatural peace. In verse 2 of the hymn, Spafford recognized part of his loss as a temptation from Satan, but then he reminded himself of Christ's great atoning death on his behalf.

Though Satan should buffet, though trials should come,
Let this blest assurance control,

That Christ has regarded my helpless estate,
And hath shed His own blood for my soul.[6]

Now Spafford could triumphantly await the glorious return of the Savior when faith would become sight! Spafford's deep sorrow in the death of his daughters was overshadowed by the redemption Christ had wrought and that would culminate one day in the triumphant return of Jesus Christ (verse 4 of his hymn).

It was well with Horatio Spafford's soul. And it can be well with our soul amid the sorrows and bad things of life. Yes, everything happens for a reason, even the loss of loved ones. Who can fathom how many lives have been helped spiritually through "It Is Well With My Soul"?

GOD'S BOUNDLESS COMFORT

God's comfort in our "bad things" is boundless. He is the God of "all" comfort, who comforts us in "all our affliction" (2 Cor. 1:4). This is the only place where true comfort will be found. Many people seek comfort in alcohol, entertainment, or a shopping spree, but there is, at most, temporary comfort in those things. True and lasting comfort cannot be found apart from the God of all comfort. Genuine comfort comes from God. It is noteworthy that the word "comfort" occurs ten times in verses 3–7. There is a purposeful emphasis on this word, reminding us that amid suffering God comforts us.

Do you have this understanding of God? Do you recognize that His nature is one of comfort—that in your trials it is His nature to minister comfort to you?

COMFORT IN ALL AFFLICTIONS

Further, God's comfort is extensive: God comforts us in "all our affliction" (2 Cor. 1:4). God doesn't say, "Well, in this I think I'll let him take it on the chin and see how he handles it by himself." No.

In *all* our sorrow, in *all* our suffering, in *all* our tragedy—in every affliction, God is there to comfort us.

The point is, God will never abandon us. People will disappoint us, circumstances will disturb us, but God will comfort us.

Some would say imprisonment is harsh suffering. How about imprisonment and death of a spouse? In 1937, before World War II, Darlene and Russell Deibler began serving Christ as missionaries in New Guinea. But with the Japanese onslaught leading to the war, Darlene, Russell, and other missionaries were placed under house arrest on March 13, 1942. Eight days later Russell and most of the men were trucked to a Japanese war camp in Pare Pare. One year later, Darlene, now herself a prisoner in Kampili, learned Russell had died in a world of physical and mental torture.

Darlene's liberation from the Japanese prison camp came on September 19, 1945. She returned to America as a twenty-eight-year-old widow, broken in spirit and physically destroyed. She had left Kampili destitute; all her personal mementos and possessions were broken. She prayed a bitter prayer: "Lord, I'll never come to these islands again. They've robbed me of everything that was dear to me."

Without the eternal perspective, Darlene seemed to be in a prison once more. Bitter, confused, and resentful, she wondered what God had done. But then she heard Indonesian voices singing—natives who had come to faith in Christ through her ministry: "God be with you till we meet again. By His counsel's guide, uphold you, With His sheep securely fold you; God be with you till we meet again."[7]

The singing of those she and her husband had served in Christ's name released her from hurt and bitterness. Through them God gave His comfort. Darlene saw God's perspective.

WE SUFFER SO WE MIGHT COMFORT OTHERS

As Chris and Samantha pointed out in their letter to friends after their daughter's early homegoing to heaven, God comforts

us "so that we may be able to comfort those who are in any affliction with the comfort with which we ourselves are comforted by
God" (v. 4). This statement clearly gives a key reason why God's
people suffer—it is so they can comfort others who are suffering.

If you have stood near the grave of a loved one, you can understand and comfort someone who is grieving over the loss of a
close family member. You can put your arm around that person
and weep with them. You can offer words of encouragement and
strength. If you have been a widow for several
years, you can comfort someone who have
been recently widowed. If you has suffered financial hardship, you can
comfort someone who is unem-
ployed. The list—and the ministry
opportunities—are endless.

After my wife died,
Buster, a widower who
knew what it was like,
came alongside me.

At no other time are such
opportunities greater than when
we lose a member of the family.
When a student's brother died, I could
offer him words of comfort because my
only brother, whom I loved very much, had
died. But after my wife died, others ministered to me. Buster, a widower who knew what it was like, came alongside me and has ministered to me in a profound way. He shared with me about grief,
what to expect, and how to handle grief and loneliness. And when
my friend Woody's wife died, I had the opportunity to minister
similarly to Woody.

GOD'S COMFORT IS ABUNDANT

Words like, "I just can't take it any longer" sometimes rever-
berate from the lips of a suffering saint. Yet a precious truth of
Scripture is that our suffering will never exceed God's comfort.

The tiny words "just as" and "so also" are significant (2 Cor. 1:5).

Just as we identify in sufferings with Christ, so also God overflows with His comfort to us. The point is clear: Our sufferings will never exceed the availability of God's comfort. His comfort will always overflow to us, exceeding our suffering.

LIVING LIFE RUSSELL PATTERSON-STYLE

Russell Patterson, a thirty-eight-year-old, successful salesman in Alabama, husband, and father of three, lived life to the fullest with an exuberant faith and love of family and life.[8] One December, when the children were hoping for a white Christmas that failed to materialize, Patterson got two truckloads of snow from the Alpine Ice Arena and dumped it onto their front yard so the children could build snowmen. His wife exclaimed, "Once you've lived life Russell–Patterson style, it's a very hard act to follow."

When Russell began stuttering and having trouble forming simple words, he realized something was wrong. On Valentine's Day the doctor informed him he had a brain tumor. "He and Dr. Marshall prayed together," Mrs. Patterson said. "From that moment, God gave him a peace, and he felt God's presence with Him." Russell Patterson had always walked the walk and "Never, ever did he feel sorry for himself. He knew that this was God's will," exclaimed his wife.

Doctors cut out a small portion of the cancer in the first operation, fearing Patterson would lose his speech with more aggressive surgery. In a second operation, five weeks later, the surgeon removed most of the tumor and inserted chemo wafers to kill the remainder of the cancer. But in the next two months a blood clot formed in his leg, and he developed pneumonia and later kidney failure. The day following his return to Duke University Medical Center, his heart stopped and doctors were unable to bring him back.

"Russell was not mine to keep," Mrs. Patterson said. "Russell was created for God's pleasure and to glorify God, and he glorified God every day of his life. . . . I was only blessed with him for 10 years.

"I knew it had to be God's plan to call Russell home—that He wanted to be with him. . . . Through all my pain that I'm having and grief and sense of loss, I have that underlying sense of peace and contentment that can only come from God."

TOUCHING OTHER LIVES

Russell Patterson's vibrant faith touched other lives—many lives. His four-hour surgery at Duke University Medical Center was telecast on The Discovery Channel and was featured on a series called *Hospital.* The producer of the series and countless others were impacted by Patterson's vibrant faith and courage.

"I've been making documentaries for fifteen years, and nobody has every touched us like the Russell Patterson family," said Bill Hayes, the producer for Advanced Medical Productions. "Russell was one of the most influential people I've ever met in my life," said Hayes, who spoke at Russell's funeral. "Here's somebody facing death and in spite of that, he never lost his sense of humor or compassion for other people. He was constantly reaching out to other people and making them feel good about themselves."[9]

Russell Patterson and his wife found God's peace and comfort filling their hearts amid their suffering. They trusted in God's sovereign plan even though they did not understand it. And their faith and peace in God helped many others in their spiritual walk. God may use our suffering as an encouragement to others and to develop them spiritually.

MODELING GOD'S GRACE

Whether Paul was afflicted or when he received comfort from God, it was for the benefit of the Corinthian believers (2 Cor. 1:4–6). Paul could in turn comfort the Corinthians with the comfort which he received from God. When Paul patiently endured his sufferings, he was a model for the Corinthians to similarly patiently endure their sufferings. The phrase "patient enduring" (v. 6; *hupomone*) has a basic meaning of "to remain under." As Rogers and Rogers amplify it, the phrase "was used in the endurance of that which has come upon man against his will. In classical [Greek] it is used also of the ability of a plant to live under hard and unfavorable circumstances. It was later used of that quality which enabled men to die for their god."[10] "It refers to . . . unyielding, defiant perseverance in the face of aggressive misfortune, and thus to a kind of courageousness."[11]

When bad things happen, believers can model the supernatural grace of God by remaining steadfast in faith and quiet trust. They become radiant witnesses of the genuineness of their faith to both believers and unbelievers alike—and who can calculate the results from a vibrant testimony? Only heaven's records will reveal the people who came to faith and the believers who were strengthened in their faith when seeing the courage of a suffering yet steadfast believer. This is especially true when we exhibit God's grace through the loss of a loved one.

EDNA'S STORY

Edna, who once worked in our church office, is a radiant believer in Jesus Christ. She enjoys the Savior's peace, a peace that is evident to all who know her. Edna has experienced bad things happening to her like very few believers will ever experience. None were more challenging than 1985.

Married with two daughters and two sons, she lost nineteen-year-old Darren to a fatal motorcycle accident.

"The pain was indescribable. Life became very difficult. There was not a minute of the day that I was not consumed with the loss of Darren. Life would never be the same."

Two months later her twenty-five-year marriage ended in divorce. "I do not believe in divorce and truly intended to keep my commitment to stay married, for better or for worse. However, when the many years of verbal abuse turned to physical abuse toward the children and [me], I felt I had to leave for our safety."

Three months after that, in September, she saw her doctor after feeling constantly tired. The doctor ordered lab work, including testing for mononucleosis. That was negative, but the blood work revealed her body was producing too many white cells.

The doctor called her in and he "was using a lot of medical terms that I did not understand," Edna recalled. "I finally asked him if this 'monster' had a name. He told me I had chronic lymphocytic leukemia."

Edna was stunned and upset. "I did not have a good attitude about the illness. I remember telling my pastor's wife that God surely must hate me. She reminded me that God loved me very much. I told her that if this was the way God showed His love, I guess I wished He wouldn't love me quite so much. God forgave me for that and began proving to me over and over that He did love me.

"Healing takes a long time. But God sent just the right people into my life to encourage me and help me through the grieving process, and to help me adjust to the many changes that were taking place in my life. Then He gave me opportunities to help others struggling along the way. That is when I really began to heal. God is so good and so faithful."[12]

She began to listen to a Christian radio station, and found strength in the messages and music. During her times in the Scriptures, "God also gave me many Bible verses that really spoke to me and encouraged me." She found great comfort in Jeremiah 29:11–13, which ends with God declaring, "Then you will call upon Me and come and pray to Me, and I will listen to you. You will seek Me and find Me when you seek Me with all your heart."

"I did begin to seek God with all of my heart," Edna says. "I did call on Him and prayed to Him; and He did listen. I found Him to be a faithful friend who cared very much for me. And I knew that

He had a wonderful plan for my life. Our lives are like a tapestry that God is weaving. We only see the backside of that tapestry but He sees the beautiful finished product. Psalm 139:15–16 says, 'My frame was not hidden from You, when I was made in the secret place, when I was woven together in the depths of the earth. Your eyes saw my unformed body; All the days ordained for me were written in Your book before one of them came to be.' [NIV]

> "In the valleys God gets our attention and draws us to Himself."

"God knew all about me. He knew me before I was even born. He knew everything I had ever said, thought, and done, and He still loved me. I cannot comprehend that kind of love."

Edna looks back at those events and says she learned much from what she calls the "valleys of life."

"No one likes to walk through the valleys of life. We would much rather jump from mountaintop to mountaintop. But it is in the valleys God gets our attention, draws us to Himself, and can begin to produce His perfect will in our lives."

Then Edna makes a remarkable statement. "If God offered to give me back Darren, restore my marriage, and take away the leukemia in exchange for the blessings He has bestowed on me since that time, I would not willingly give up what I have gained for what I thought I had lost.

"Yes, I do miss Darren. I still shed many tears for him. I probably always will. But I believe with all of my heart that he is in heaven, because as a young man he gave his heart to Jesus. And I believe I will see him again some day."

The valley may not be as deep, but there are still shadows of uncertainty in Edna's life, although worry does not linger in the shadows. Edna writes:

I still have leukemia, but I am not worrying about it. God is still in control and He knows what is best for me. I am just going to keep on telling as many people as I can that God loves them and He has a wonderful plan for their lives. If you are walking through the valley, be encouraged, my friend. God is faithful; you can trust Him with your life. . . . There can be peace in the valley.[13]

Edna's joy and victory amid enormous suffering has been an inspiration to many who work with her and know her. And Edna has brought glory to God amid her suffering. Whether it is the death of a member of our own family or someone else's loved one, God often uses the loss to give us comfort. Always He uses such suffering for His glory and to show His care. Sometimes the difficulties we experience are there for the benefit of others—to show them the power of God and the grace of God in sustaining and strengthening a believer in very difficult situations. In the process we are challenged to mature in Christ by a quiet trust in God's mysterious and sovereign ways.

"God is faithful. There can be peace in the valley."

Yes, everything happens for a reason—whether or not we see it or recognize it.

11

The Ultimate Resolution

We were all sitting around the kitchen table when the phone call came. My brother-in-law answered the phone, and when he returned to the kitchen, he announced, "It's all over." My father had died. At the age of forty-eight he lived to be the oldest of his nine siblings. He had outlived his mother (my grandmother) by a scant three years.

In God's mercy, my mother had been with my father shortly before he died. At his request she read Psalm 23 to him. He also meditated on a favorite verse: "Truly, truly, I say to you, he who hears My word, and believes Him who sent Me, has eternal life, and does not come into judgment, but has passed out of death into life" (John 5:24). My father's short, earthly life had ended, and he had passed from death into life and into the presence of His Savior.

But from an earthly perspective, the ultimate bad thing had happened to my mother with the death of my father. A young widow of forty-six, my mother was ill prepared to function alone. She was very dependent on my father, and when he died, her world collapsed.

Both my mother and father were believers in Jesus Christ and took refuge in Him. Weighed on the scale of human values, my father's early death was a tragedy. My mother was widowed for nearly twice as many years as she was married. I had my father for a short nine years—a father I loved, admired, and needed—but he was gone.

So how can we evaluate this ultimate bad thing that happened? Was there a reason for his early homegoing? We cannot consider it from an earthly perspective alone. For the believer, the good and bad cannot be evaluated from what happens in this life.

INCOMPARABLE FUTURE GLORY

When we think of bad things happening to God's people, we think of things happening to us in *this* life. The entire focus of our concern is this life—here and now. But that is incorrect thinking. The span of our threescore and ten on this earth (see Psalm 90:10) is but a slight sliver of time when eternity is considered. Our earthly sufferings must be weighed against heaven's glories. That will put the issues of life in perspective. Our life does not consist only of our earthly existence. We are eternal, and the drama of our earthly events must be evaluated alongside a heavenly perspective. Only then will we come to terms with the difficulties of this life.

The apostle Paul reminds us, "For I consider that the sufferings of this present time are not worthy to be compared with the glory that is to be revealed to us" (Rom. 8:18). This life, with all its suffering, is but a brief, pale shadow across our path, while the brilliant light and glory of God's eternal bliss will shine down on us forever. In considering this glorious prospect, Paul exclaimed that we are "heirs of God and fellow heirs with Christ, if indeed we suffer with Him so that we may also be glorified with Him" (v. 17).

As believers we are joined to Christ; hence, in this life we walk the road that He walked—which includes suffering. There is a distinct purpose for our suffering in this life. The phrase "so that" (v. 17) reminds us that the suffering is the necessary prelude to the glory. Every believer in Jesus Christ will share His glory for *all eternity*. That is where the ultimate resolution will be found. Heaven will provide the reason for the things that happen to us.

The apostle Peter provides similar words of encouragement. Speaking to believers who were suffering severe persecution, he exclaimed, "In this [glorification at Christ's return] you greatly rejoice, even though now for a little while, if necessary, you have been distressed by various trials, so that the proof of your faith, being more precious than gold which is perishable, even though tested by fire, may be found to result in praise and glory and honor at the revelation of Jesus Christ" (1 Peter 1:6–7). Trials are temporary; eternal glory with Christ is permanent. Suffering, even death, cannot rob believers of the glorious future that awaits them.

> Heaven will provide the reason for the things that happen to us.

A YOUNG, EFFECTIVE MISSIONARY

Dan was a young missionary serving the Lord with Word of Life in Hungary. His spirited, dedicated leadership was highly effective in attracting young people to the gospel. He was loved and respected and had a significant ministry to the youth of Hungary. Dan had also discovered the one whom he believed God had brought into his life to be his wife. Dan was engaged to be married.

On May 1, 1996, as Dan was driving his car around the new Budapest bypass, a Coca-Cola truck pulling a trailer was traveling toward him. As the truck approached, the trailer became unhitched from the truck and veered into Dan's path, hitting his car at the windshield level. Although Dan lived for another ten days, the injury proved fatal and Dan died.[1]

Humanly speaking, it is difficult to understand a death like Dan's. He was a young, dedicated Christian leader, highly effective in ministry on the mission field. Yet, in the sovereign will of God, the Lord took him home. Why did the Lord allow Dan to die so early in life when he was being used so effectively in ministry?

Ultimately, the answer lies with God. We cannot know the mind of God; He alone is all-wise and entirely good. We can only speculate—and that is not always advisable. We do know that within a short time over forty young people came to faith in Jesus Christ because of the testimony Dan left behind. And the story is not over. What about those forty? How many will they bring to the Lord in the months and years that follow? And what of the renewed courage for the missionaries and workers at Word of Life? How has it impacted them to renewed vigor in evangelism, to take up the torch from Dan and continue his ministry?

The answer lies with the Lord, but we can see the immediate harvest of souls and invigorated ministry because of Dan's testimony.

FAITHFULNESS AND FUTURE GLORY

Paul knew of his impending death when he penned the words of 2 Timothy. He could say, "I have fought the good fight, I have finished the course, I have kept the faith; in the future there is laid up for me the crown of righteousness, which the Lord, the righteous Judge, will award to me on that day; and not only to me, but also to all who have loved His appearing" (4:7–8). From God's perspective Dan had completed his course; he had kept the faith and had communicated the faith to the young people at Word of Life in Toalmas, Hungary. Dan awaited the crown of righteousness, which he would receive from the Lord on that day. He had been faithful to the stewardship entrusted to him.

Paul concluded his epistle with the hopeful words: "The Lord will deliver me from every evil deed, and will bring me safely to His heavenly kingdom; to Him be the glory forever and ever. Amen" (v. 18). The Lord ultimately delivers believers from the evils of the enemy who opposes the gospel. The Lord brings His own safely into His kingdom. The thought brought Paul into an ecstacy of praise: "to Him be the glory forever and ever."

Suffering and tragedy in this life allow Christians to rejoice as they anticipate the coming glory with Christ. Paul was confident that his temporary sufferings on earth would issue in the glorious heavenly kingdom of Christ. That can be our confidence and hope as well.

A MINISTRY CURTAILED

On June 15, 2000, James Montgomery Boice, senior minister of Tenth Presbyterian Church in Philadelphia, died of liver cancer. A prominent evangelical leader, Dr. Boice had a wide ministry that impacted many listeners and readers. He had seen his congregation grow from 350 to 1,200 during his tenure of thirty-two years. Since 1969 he was the teacher on *The Bible Study Hour* program, which was broadcast on more than 238 radio stations. He also served as president of the Alliance of Confessing Evangelicals, and he wrote many books.

Committed to the inerrancy of the Scriptures, Dr. Boice provided prominent leadership as chairman with the International Council on Biblical Inerrancy from its founding in 1977 until the completion of its work in 1988.

Dr. Boice was a prolific writer, supplying pastors and teachers with notable volumes of biblical exposition—commentaries on Genesis, John, Philippians, the Sermon on the Mount, and numerous others that flowed from his pen. A strong biblicist, he sounded the biblical alarm as he exposed the weaknesses of modern evangelicalism.

But Dr. Boice died at the relatively young age of sixty-one.

Unquestionably, Dr. Boice's death has left a void in evangelical leadership. But it is not for us to question God's wisdom or God's sovereignty. God never makes mistakes. Upon learning of his fatal disease, Dr. Boice himself said to his congregation, "If God does something in your life, would you change it? If you'd change it, you'd make it worse. It wouldn't be as good."[2]

DEATH IS GAIN

Boice knew everything has a reason, even an early death. There is a reason for everything because God is both sovereign and good. Still we cannot explain many things that God permits. Surely the early death of a loved one is one of those things. Whether a family member or close friend dies early or after a long, full life, there is real loss. There is the pain of separation, the earthly loss of a loved one. As we noted in chapter 10, the sorrow and grief in losing a loved one is an unparalleled earthly experience. This side of heaven we will never see the loved one again. Most everyone has stood at a graveside and wept as the body of a loved one was lowered into the heart of the earth.

When we consider the "bad things," happening to God's people, certainly death is the ultimate "bad thing," from a human perspective. Yet let's remember that from a biblical perspective it is not loss but gain for the believer. Paul's pointed statement reminds us that "to die is gain" (Phil. 1:21). But the last part of this statement is connected with the first part, "For to me, to live is Christ." The believer who has lived for Christ finds death to be gain.

"To die is gain" envisions the consequences of death. For the believer, death is profitable because it continues the life of fellowship with Christ. Moreover, we will see Christ in all His glory— the One who gave Himself for us.

If we recognize that our departed loved one is with Christ, basking in Christ's presence, seeing Him face to face and worshiping Him, it will comfort us in our sorrow.

But you may say, "My loved one has died and was not a Christian. What hope is there for me?" An important thing to remember is that God is good and God is just. He will do what is right. When you get to glory, you will agree with the Lord that He did what is right and there will be no heartache. Further, you do not know what happened to your loved one moments before he or she died.

> From pain to paradise! From sorrow to the Savior's presence!

One Christian lady asked me to come see her unsaved husband who was dying. As I arrived, he was in a coma. I stood beside his bed and carefully and clearly explained the gospel to him and told him simply to believe in his heart the message that he heard. He died shortly after that. Was he saved? Possibly. If he heard me, he simply, in the quietness of his heart could have believed the message, and he would have been saved. You do not know what happened to your unsaved loved one the moment he or she departed this life. Perhaps they recalled the gospel they had heard and believed it while departing. The repentant thief at Calvary believed even as He was dying and was promised paradise that day (Luke 23:39–43). Remember, God is love (1 John 4:8), and God is righteous and true (Rev. 15:3) He will do what is right, and you can be at peace. You and I can rest in that truth.

LOOKING TOWARD THE END OF ALL PAIN

We all have loved ones or friends who have undergone horrible suffering in this life before they died. No one would dare minimize the pain of bone cancer, leukemia, or other painful diseases that may precede death. Yet as we study the crucifixion of our Savior and learn of the horrors of Roman scourging, and other terrible tortures associated with His earthly death, we discover a key truth about pain and dying.

Jesus hung on the cross between two thieves—both of whom had been lacerated by the Roman scourging. In the midst of His own pain, Jesus spoke words of comfort and hope to the penitent thief. Ringing loud above the pain of the torn body, were the words of Christ: "Truly I say to you, today you shall be with Me in Paradise" (Luke 23:43). From pain to paradise! From sorrow to the Savior's presence!

The believer's death must be understood in that sense. As a young pastor in western Canada, I was often encouraged when Earl Longwell came from southern California to visit his daughter. Earl and his wife, Ruth, would also visit our home, and we always sensed the presence of Christ with both of them. Fellowship with Christ was a reality to them.

Several years passed when one day Earl called me. When I inquired about Ruth, Earl exclaimed, "Oh, she went home to be with the Lord."

"Oh, I'm sorry to hear that," I responded.

"Oh, don't say that," he said. "When I think of her, that she is in the presence of Christ, I get so happy for her, I almost feel guilty that I am not sorrowing as I should."

Earl understood the reality of the biblical words, "to die is gain," "to be absent from the body is to be present with the Lord," and "You shall be with Me in Paradise." Earl knew Ruth was in the presence of the Lord and she was rejoicing in her Savior. That is how we must understand the believer's death. Yes, from a human perspective there is pain and sorrow, but from the divine, eternal perspective there is everlasting joy and bliss. That *is* the reality.

SORROW AMID HOPE

When Paul explained the resurrection to the Thessalonian believers, he reminded them, "We do not want you to be uninformed, brethren, about those who are asleep [have died], so that you will not grieve, as do the rest who have no hope" (1 Thess. 4:13). Several things are noteworthy. One is that believers do sorrow. Tears are shed when a loved one dies. It is natural and it is right. Jesus wept at the grave of Lazarus (John 11:35). But the believer's sorrow is different from an unbeliever's.

The believer weeps *amid* hope when a loved one dies. Paul explains the reason for the hope: "For if [since] we believe that Jesus died and rose again, even so God will bring with Him those who have fallen asleep in Jesus" (1 Thess. 4:14). The encouragement is clear: Because Jesus rose again after He died, when He returns He will also bring with Him those who have died believing in Jesus. *Death is not the end!* Earthly life is the end! Our loved ones will live again.

When Christ returns, the bodies of departed believers will be resurrected and transformed, with new bodies; and living believers will be transformed and reunited with them to be with the Lord forever. This is a great word of comfort (v. 18). We must remind ourselves in our sorrow that death is not the end. Reunion and everlasting life in the presence of the Savior—that is our glorious future and end!

OUR TRUE HOME

As the old gospel song says, "This world is not my home; I'm just a passin' through."[3] Indeed, we are strangers and pilgrims, passing through this world on our way to the celestial city. Believers "desire a better country, that is, a heavenly one. Therefore God is not ashamed to be called their God; for He has prepared a city for them" (Heb. 11:16).

Perhaps it is because we have let our roots sink too deep into this world; perhaps we have been captivated by the spirit of this world and when a loved one dies, we see it from the perspective of this world. If this world is all that we hope in, then death is a great tragedy and a loss. But if we, like Abraham, are looking for the city of God and a better country (see Hebrews 11:10), then all is not lost in death. Death merely becomes the believers' transition to a better place, a glorious home that Christ has prepared for them that love Him (John 14:2).

D. L. MOODY ON HEAVEN

Dwight L. Moody, the great nineteenth-century evangelist and one of the Lord's choicest servants, had a great longing for heaven.

In one of his last sermons, Moody poignantly contrasted the suffering and sadness in this life with the joy, happiness, and bliss of an eternal heaven:

> We say this is the land of the living! It is not. It is the land of the dying. What is our life here but a vapour? A hearse is the most common sight. . . . Over there is one who has lost a father, there a mother, there is a place vacant, there a sister's name is no more heard, there a brother's love is missed. Death stalks triumphant through our midst, in this world. . . . Death in front of us, death behind us, death to the right of us, death to the left of us. . . .
>
> But look at the other world. No death, no pain, no sorrow, no old age, no sickness, no bending forms, no dimmed eyes, no tears. But joy, peace, love, happiness. No grey hair. People all young. River of life for the healing of the nations, and everlasting life. Think of it! Life! Life! Life without end! And yet so many men choose this life on earth, instead of the life in heaven.[4]

Heaven was real to Dwight L. Moody. He spoke confidently of his assurance of a joyous life with Christ for all eternity. He commented:

Some day you will read in the papers that D. L. Moody of East Northfield is dead. Don't you believe a word of it! At that moment I shall be more alive than I am now. I shall have gone up higher, that is all—out of this old clay tenement into a house that is immortal; a body that death cannot touch, that sin cannot taint, a body fashioned like unto His glorious body.[5]

NO DEATH—EVER!

Jesus resolved mankind's greatest dilemma when He spoke His words of hope to Martha: "I am the resurrection, and the life; he who believes in Me shall live even if he dies, and everyone who lives and believes in Me shall never die" (John 11:25–26). These words are entirely reliable and trustworthy. Their truthfulness is conditioned on the integrity of Jesus. Is Jesus reliable? Are His words trustworthy? Indeed they are. Then we can rest in the promises of John 11:25–26.

This is the ultimate resolution to our ultimate dilemma, death. Our redemption and rescue from sin's judgment is eternal life with Christ. Jesus reminds Martha that He is the resurrection— He will resurrect our physical bodies on that climactic day. But He also reminds her—and us—that there is a true sense in which we will never die. "Everyone who lives and believes in Me shall never die," he says. Physically, we will die because we will lay aside this body of corruption, but spiritually we will never die. We will simply transition to heaven when the Lord calls us.

At death, we put off this temporary tent in order that we might be clothed with immortality (2 Cor. 5:4). This body is like a tent that is folded up upon death; its usefulness has been completed. But after we put aside this earthly tent, we will have a "building from God" (v. 1), a glorified, eternal body. That is God's resolution to man's great dilemma.

Scripture reminds us that "our Savior Christ Jesus . . . abolished death and brought life and immortality to light through the gospel" (2 Tim. 1:10). What a profound statement! "Abolished" (*katargesantos*) means "to render inoperative, to make inactive, to annul."[6] Death is annulled, rendered inoperative. Jesus Christ has destroyed death and brought believers life! And we await the final aspect of this phenomenal truth at the resurrection.

> In our resurrection body the capacity to sin will be gone. There will no longer be any suffering due to sin.

Unlike our perishable earthly body, our resurrection body will be imperishable, no longer subject to decay or control by sin. This is the final resolution to our earthly struggles and sufferings. Think of it! The capacity to sin will be gone. There will no longer be any suffering due to sin. But neither will our resurrection bodies be subject to decay. Our glorified bodies will be constant in health and vitality. What a prospect! And that will continue for all eternity. That will place a shadow of forgetfulness on all earthly suffering.

A MARVELOUS NEW BODY

Our resurrection bodies will be like the resurrection body of Jesus Christ Himself. Jesus was recognizable in His resurrection body, indicating it was the same material body that He had during His earthly ministry. When Jesus spoke to Mary, she recognized Him (John 20:16). When the eyes of the disciples on the road to Emmaus were opened, they recognized the Savior (Luke 24:31). Jesus reminded the apostles that He was not simply a spirit; He had a body of flesh and bones (v. 39). Moreover, the nail prints in His hands and the wound in His side revealed that His resurrection body had a continuity with His earthly body (John 20:20, 25). It was the same material body of His earthly life but it was glorified.

Ultimately, everyone will die physically (except those alive when Jesus returns), so the resolution to the dilemma cannot be in this life. For the unbeliever it remains unresolved because he has refused God's gracious gift in His Son, Jesus Christ, who has made atonement for man's sin, removing the barrier between a holy God and sinful man. The unbeliever faces a bleak and horrid eternity. But for the believer, death is not a tragedy; it is a coronation and a promotion to a higher place of life—eternal life of fellowship with the triune God. The believer in Christ looks for the better place, the celestial city, where Christ is, and where there is a reunion of loved ones who have gone before.

In heaven, God "will dwell among them, and they shall be his people, and God Himself will be among them, and He will wipe away every tear from their eyes; and there will no longer be any death; there will no longer be any mourning, or crying, or pain; the first things have passed away" (Rev. 21:3–4).

The joy and glories of heaven are incomparable to anything in this life. Nor can the sufferings of this life be compared with the joy of heaven (Rom. 8:18). No matter how much we or our loved ones suffer in this life, it is incomparable with the riches of the believer's inheritance in Christ.

On that future day, God will wipe away all tears. Tears come because of sorrow, pain, grief, and sin. But heaven will know none of these. No longer will there be illness, sickness, and death. Believers will be eternal citizens of the new heaven and new earth, devoid of all suffering or sadness.

GOD'S SOVEREIGN PLAN FOR HIS PEOPLE

The ultimate resolution to sin and death will come with our arrival in heaven, where God the Father and Son are. At present, humanity remains subject to suffering, sickness, tragedy, and death. No generation, no race, no ethnic group has been exempt from suffering. Because believers live in this fallen world, they too experience suffering. Nonetheless, they are the objects of God's sovereign love and grace; they are in His plan to culminate the ages for His glory.

In the outworking of history, God has a sovereign plan for His people amid their earthly existence. Things do not happen at random to God's people. Everything has a reason. Bad things may happen to believers because of Satan's attacks or because of believers' sins. But bad things may also happen to believers to comfort, strengthen, and encourage other believers—and sometimes bad things happen for the believer's own spiritual maturing.

Why bad things happen to God's people will ultimately be resolved in eternity—and there we will recognize that everything happens for a reason.

12

The Present Solution

There are several summary things to do when suffering and loss come your way. First, *remember that God is sovereign*. He controls all events that transpire, although He is never the author of evil (Eph. 1:11). That understanding brings great comfort.

Second, *think the right thoughts*. Dwelling on the suffering and the tragedies that happen can be devastating. Our thoughts need to be centered on Jesus Christ and the blessings we enjoy through our union with Him (Eph. 1:3–12; Col. 3:1–4).

Third, *to encourage right thinking* amid the trials of life, *nurture a divine perspective of the issues*. You will receive strength, encouragement, and comfort by reflecting on God's Word.

MEDITATE ON THE SCRIPTURES

It is vital that we not only read, but meditate on the Scriptures. To meditate involves reflection and contemplation on the meaning and implications of the Scriptures.

The following Scriptures are topically arranged. Read, meditate and reflect on these (and others) for encouragement and strength. These are only a beginning. The Bible is rich with instructive, encouraging, and comforting words. Read the Bible and write down verses of encouragement that you find on your own reading and study.

Burdens

Cast your burden upon the Lord and He will sustain you; He will never allow the righteous to be shaken. —PSALM 55:22

Blessed be the Lord, who daily bears our burden, the God who is our salvation. —PSALM 68:19

· ·

Blessing

For the Lord God is a sun and shield; the Lord gives grace and glory; no good thing does He withhold from those who walk uprightly. O Lord of hosts, how blessed is the man who trusts in You! —PSALM 84:11–12

Bless the Lord, O my soul, and all that is within me, bless His holy name. Bless the Lord, O my soul, and forget none of His benefits; Who pardons all your iniquities, Who heals all your diseases; Who redeems your life from the pit, Who crowns you with lovingkindness and compassion; Who satisfies your years with good things, so that your youth is renewed like the eagle. —PSALM 103:1–5

Blessed be the God and Father of our Lord Jesus Christ, who has blessed us with every spiritual blessing in the heavenly places in Christ. —EPHESIANS 1:3

· ·

Christ: Knowing Him

I pray that the eyes of your heart may be enlightened, so that you will know what is the hope of His calling, what are the

riches of the glory of His inheritance in the saints, and what
is the surpassing greatness of His power toward us who
believe. —EPHESIANS 1:18–19a

I count all things to be loss in view of the surpassing value of
knowing Christ Jesus my Lord, for whom I have suffered the
loss of all things, and count them but rubbish so that I may
gain Christ. —PHILIPPIANS 3:8

That I may know Him and the power of His resurrection and
the fellowship of His sufferings, being conformed to His
death. —PHILIPPIANS 3:10

. . . .

Christ: Riches in Him
In everything you were enriched in Him. —1 CORINTHIANS 1:5

In Him we have redemption through His blood, the forgiveness of our trespasses, according to the riches of His grace.
—EPHESIANS 1:7

That He would grant you, according to the riches of His glory,
to be strengthened with power through His Spirit in the inner
man. —EPHESIANS 3:16

And My God will supply all your needs according to His riches
in glory in Christ Jesus. —PHIIPPIANS 4:19

. . . .

Christ Satisfies
"I am the bread of life; he who comes to Me will not hunger,
and he who believes in Me will never thirst." —JOHN 6:35

"If anyone is thirsty, let him come to Me and drink. He who
believes in Me, as the Scripture said, 'From his innermost being will flow rivers of living water.'" —JOHN 7:37–38

"I am the door; if anyone enters through Me, he will be
saved, and will go in and out and find pasture. . . . I came that
they may have life, and have it abundantly." —JOHN 10:9, 10

"I am the vine, you are the branches; he who abides in Me and I in him, he bears much fruit, for apart from me you can do nothing." —JOHN 15:5

. . . .

Comfort
Blessed be the God and Father of our Lord Jesus Christ, the Father of mercies and God of all comfort, who comforts us in all our affliction so that we will be able to comfort those who are in any affliction with the comfort with which we ourselves are comforted by God. —2 CORINTHIANS 1:3–4

Now may our Lord Jesus Christ Himself and God our Father, who has loved us and given us eternal comfort and good hope by grace, comfort and strengthen your hearts in every good work and word. —2 THESSALONIANS 2:16–17

. . . .

Contentment
I have learned to be content in whatever circumstances I am.
—PHILIPPIANS 4:11

But godliness actually is a means of great gain when accompanied by contentment. For we have brought nothing into the world, so we cannot take anything out of it either.
—1 TIMOTHY 6:6–7

Make sure that your character is free from the love of money, being content with what you have; for He Himself has said, "I will never desert you, nor will I ever forsake you."
—HEBREWS 13:5

. . . .

Courage
"Be strong and courageous, do not be afraid or tremble at them, for the Lord your God is the one who goes with you. He will not fail you or forsake you." —DEUTERONOMY 31:6

"Have I not commanded you? Be strong and courageous! Do not tremble or be dismayed, for the Lord your God is with you wherever you go." —JOSHUA 1:9

Wait for the Lord; be strong and let your heart take courage; yes, wait for the Lord. —PSALM 27:14

. . . .

Death

"I am the resurrection and the life; he who believes in Me will live even if he dies, and everyone who lives and believes in Me will never die." —JOHN 11:25–26

We are of good courage, I say, and prefer rather to be absent from the body and to be at home with the Lord.
—2 CORINTHIANS 5:8

For to me, to live is Christ and to die is gain. —PHILIPPIANS 1:21

But I am hard-pressed from both directions, having the desire to depart and be with Christ, for that is very much better.
—PHILIPPIANS 1:23

. . . .

Despair

Why are you in despair, O my soul? And why have you become disturbed within me? Hope in God, for I shall again praise Him for the help of His presence. —PSALM 42:5

. . . .

Disappointment

He who believes in Him [Christ] will not be disappointed.
—1 PETER 2:6b

. . . .

Discipline

And you have forgotten the exhortation which is addressed to you as sons, "My son, do not regard lightly the discipline of the Lord, nor faint when you are reproved by Him; for those whom the Lord loves He disciplines, and He scourges every son whom He receives." . . . All discipline for the moment seems not to be joyful, but sorrowful; yet to those who have been trained by it, afterwards it yields the peaceful fruit of righteousness. —Hebrews 12:5, 6, 11

* *

Endurance

Therefore, since we have so great a cloud of witnesses surrounding us, let us also lay aside every encumbrance and the sin which so easily entangles us, and let us run with endurance the race that is set before us, fixing our eyes on Jesus, the author and perfecter of faith, who for the joy set before Him endured the cross, despising the shame, and has sat down at the right hand of the throne of God.

—Hebrews 12:1–2

Consider it all joy, my brethren, when you encounter various trials, knowing that the testing of your faith produces endurance. And let endurance have its perfect result, so that you may be perfect and complete, lacking in nothing.
—James 1:2–4

* *

Example

For you have been called for this purpose, since Christ also suffered for you, leaving you an example for you to follow in His steps. —1 Peter 2:21

* *

Faith

"If you have faith the size of a mustard seed, you will say to this mountain, 'Move from here to there,' and it will move; and nothing will be impossible to you." —Matthew 17:20

"Therefore I say to you, all things for which you pray and ask, believe that you have received them, and they will be granted you." —MARK 11:24

Now faith is the assurance of things hoped for, the conviction of things not seen. . . . And without faith it is impossible to please Him, for he who comes to God must believe that He is and that He is a rewarder of those who seek Him.
—HEBREWS 11:1, 6

. . . .

Faithfulness of God

God is faithful, through whom you were called into fellowship with His Son, Jesus Christ our Lord. —1 CORINTHIANS 1:9

Faithful is He who calls you, and He also will bring it to pass.
—1 THESSALONIANS 5:24

But the Lord is faithful, and He will strengthen and protect you from the evil one. —2 THESSALONIANS 3:3

. . . .

Fear

God is our refuge and strength, a very present help in trouble. Therefore we will not fear, though the earth should change and though the mountains slip into the heart of the sea; though its waters roar and foam, though the mountains quake at its swelling pride. —PSALM 46:1–3

When I am afraid, I will put my trust in You. In God, whose word I praise, in God I have put my trust; I shall not be afraid. What can mere man do to me? —PSALM 56:3–4

"Do not fear, for I am with you; do not anxiously look about you, for I am your God. I will strengthen you, surely I will help you, surely I will uphold you with My righteous right hand."
—ISAIAH 41:10

. . . .

Forgiveness of God

When you were dead in your transgressions and the uncircumcision of your flesh, He made you alive together with Him, having forgiven us all our transgressions.
—Colossians 2:13

As far as the east is from the west, so far has He removed our transgressions from us. —Psalm 103:12

If we confess our sins, He is faithful and righteous to forgive us our sins and to cleanse us from all unrighteousness.
—1 John 1:9

. . . .

Forgiving Each Other

Be kind to one another, tender-hearted, forgiving each other, just as God in Christ also has forgiven you. —Ephesians 4:32

Bearing with one another, and forgiving each other, whoever has a complaint against anyone, just as the Lord forgave you, so also should you. —Colossians 3:13

. . . .

God: His Goodness

How great is Your goodness, which You have stored up for those who fear You, which You have wrought for those who take refuge in You, before the sons of men! You hide them in the secret place of Your presence from the conspiracies of man. —Psalm 31:19–20

O taste and see that the Lord is good; how blessed is the man who takes refuge in Him! —Psalm 34:8

Give thanks to the Lord, for He is good, for His lovingkindness is everlasting. —Psalm 136:1

. . . .

God: His Greatness

For the Lord your God is the God of gods and the Lord of
lords, the great, the mighty, and the awesome God.
—DEUTERONOMY 10:17

Great is our Lord and abundant in strength. —PSALM 147:5

. . . .

God: His Presence

Be strong and courageous, do not be afraid or tremble at
them, for the Lord your God is the one who goes with you.
He will not fail you or forsake you. —DEUTERONOMY 31:6

. . . .

Grace

For of His [Christ's] fullness we have all received,
and grace upon grace. —JOHN 1:16

And He has said to me, "My grace is sufficient for you, for
power is perfected in weakness." Most gladly, therefore, I will
rather boast about my weaknesses, so that the power of
Christ may dwell in me. Therefore I am well content with
weaknesses, with insults, with distresses, with persecutions,
with difficulties, for Christ's sake; for when I am weak, then
I am strong. —2 CORINTHIANS 12:9–10

Since then we have a great high priest who has passed
through the heavens, Jesus the Son of God, let us hold fast
our confession. For we do not have a high priest who cannot
sympathize with our weaknesses, but One who has been
tempted in all things as we are, yet without sin. Therefore let
us draw near with confidence to the throne of grace, so that
we may receive mercy and find grace to help in time of need.
—HEBREWS 4:14–16

. . . .

Guidance

For such is God, our God forever and ever; He will guide us until death. —PSALM 48:14

With Your counsel You will guide me, and afterward receive me to glory. —PSALM 73:24

When he puts forth all his own, he goes before them, and the sheep follow him because they know his voice.
—JOHN 10:4

* *

Heaven

And I heard a loud voice from the throne, saying, "Behold, the tabernacle of God is among men, and He will dwell among them, and they shall be His people, and God Himself will be among them, and He will wipe away every tear from their eyes; and there will no longer be any death; there will no longer be any mourning, or crying, or pain; the first things have passed away." —REVELATION 21:3–4

* *

Help

God is our refuge and strength, a very present help in trouble. —PSALM 46:1

Behold, God is my helper; the Lord is the sustainer of my soul. —PSALM 54:4

For You have been my help, and in the shadow of Your wings I sing for joy. My soul clings to You; Your right hand upholds me. —PSALM 63:7–8

* *

Holy Spirit: Helper and Comforter

"I will ask the Father, and He will give you another Helper, that He may be with you forever." —JOHN 14:16

"But the Helper, the Holy Spirit, whom the Father will send in My name, He will teach you all things, and bring to your remembrance all that I said to you." —John 14:26

. . . .

Hope

Now may the God of hope fill you with all joy and peace in believing, so that you will abound in hope by the power of the Holy Spirit. —Romans 15:13

. . . .

Joy

Weeping may last for the night, but a shout of joy comes in the morning. —Psalm 30:5b

"These things I have spoken to you so that My joy may be in you, and that your joy may be made full." —John 15:11

"Until now you have asked for nothing in My name; ask and you will receive, so that your joy may be made full."
—John 16:24

And though you have not seen Him, you love Him, and though you do not see Him now, but believe in Him, you greatly rejoice with joy inexpressible and full of glory.
—1 Peter 1:8

. . . .

Life

You will make known to me the path of life; in Your presence is fullness of joy; in Your right hand there are pleasures forever. —Psalm 16:11

"I came that they may have life, and have it abundantly."
—John 10:10b

. . . .

Life: Planned

Since his days are determined, the number of his months is
with You; and his limits You have set so that he cannot pass.
—Job 14:5

My times are in Your hand. —Psalm 31:15

Your eyes have seen my unformed substance; and in Your
book were all written the days that were ordained for me,
when as yet there was not one of them. —Psalm 139:16

. . . .

The Love of Christ

For I am convinced that neither death, nor life, nor angels, nor
principalities, nor things present, nor things to come, nor
powers, nor height, nor depth, nor any other created thing,
will be able to separate us from the love of God, which is in
Christ Jesus our Lord. —Romans 8:38–39

For the love of Christ controls us. —2 Corinthians 5:14

. . . .

The Lovingkindness of the Lord

Surely goodness and lovingkindness will follow me all
the days of my life, and I will dwell in the house
of the Lord forever. — Psalm 23:6

All the paths of the Lord are lovingkindness and truth to
those who keep His covenant and His testimonies.
—Psalm 25:10

The Lord will command His lovingkindness in the daytime;
and His song will be with me in the night, a prayer
to the God of my life. —Psalm 42:8

. . . .

Meditate on the Scriptures

"This book of the law shall not depart from your mouth, but
you shall meditate on it day and night, so that you may be

careful to do according to all that is written in it; for then
you will make your way prosperous, and then you will
have success." —Joshua 1:8

But his delight is in the law of the Lord, and in His law he
meditates day and night. He will be like a tree firmly planted
by streams of water, which yields its fruit in its season and its
leaf does not wither; and in whatever he does, he prospers.
—Psalm 1:2–3

O how I love Your law! It is my meditation all the day.
—Psalm 119:97

. . . .

The Mercy of God
But You, O Lord, are a God merciful and gracious, slow to
anger and abundant in lovingkindness and truth.
—Psalm 86:15

The Lord is gracious and merciful; slow to anger and great in
lovingkindness. The Lord is goodto all, and His mercies are
over all His works. —Psalm 145:8–9

. . . .

Patience
Wait for the Lord; be strong and let your heart take courage;
yes, wait for the Lord. —Psalm 27:14

Rest in the Lord and wait patiently for Him. —Psalm 37:7a

. . . .

Peace
"Peace I leave with you; My peace I give to you; not as
the world gives do I give to you. Do not let your heart be
troubled, nor let it be fearful." —John 14:27

"These things I have spoken to you, so that in Me you may
have peace. In the world you have tribulation, but take
courage; I have overcome the world." —John 16:33

Be anxious for nothing, but in everything by prayer and supplication with thanksgiving let your requests be made known to God. And the peace of God, which surpasses all comprehension, will guard your hearts and your minds in Christ Jesus. —PHILIPPIANS 4:6–7

Let the peace of Christ rule in your hearts, to which indeed you were called in one body; and be thankful.
—COLOSSIANS 3:15

Now may the Lord of peace Himself continually grant you peace in every circumstance. —2 THESSALONIANS 3:16

. . . .

Perseverance/Endurance
We also exult in our tribulations, knowing that tribulation brings about perseverance. —ROMANS 5:3

For you have need of endurance, so that when you have done the will of God, you may receive what was promised.
—HEBREWS 10:36

Therefore, since we have so great a cloud of witnesses sur-rounding us, let us also lay aside every encumbrance and the sin which so easily entangles us, and let us run with en-durance the race that is set before us, fixing our eyes on Je-sus, the author and perfecter of faith, who for the joy set be-fore Him endured the cross, despising the shame, and has sat down at the right hand of the throne of God. For consider him who has endured such hostility by sinners against Him-self, so that you will not grow weary and lose heart.
—Hebrews 12:1–3

The testing of your faith produces endurance. —James 1:3

. . . .

Prayer: Conditions for Answers
"If you abide in Me, and My words abide in you, ask whatever you wish, and it will be done for you." —JOHN 15:7

But he must ask in faith without any doubting, for the one who doubts is like the surf of the sea, driven and tossed by the wind. —JAMES 1:6

This is the confidence which we have before Him, that, if we ask anything according to His will, He hears us. —1 JOHN 5:14

. . . .

Prayer: God Answers

The Lord is near to all who call upon Him, to all who call upon Him in truth. He will fulfill the desire of those who fear Him; He will also hear their cry and will save them. —PSALM 145:18–19

"Ask, and it will be given to you; seek, and you will find; knock, and it will be opened to you. For everyone who asks receives, and he who seeks finds, and to him who knocks it will be opened." —MATTHEW 7:7–8

"Whatever you ask in My name, that will I do, so that the Father may be glorified in the Son. If you ask Me anything in My name, I will do it." —JOHN 14:13–14

The effective prayer of a righteous man can accomplish much. —JAMES 5:16b

For the eyes of the Lord are toward the righteous, and His ears attend to their prayer. —1 PETER 3:12

. . . .

Protection

Keep me as the apple of the eye; hide me in the shadow of Your wings. —PSALM 17:8

He who dwells in the shelter of the Most High will abide in the shadow of the Almighty. I will say to the Lord, "My refuge and my fortress, my God, in whom I trust."
— PSALM 91:1–2

The Lord will protect you from all evil; He will keep your soul. The Lord will guard your going out and your coming in from this time forth and forever. —PSALM 121:7–8

The name of the Lord is a strong tower; the righteous
runs into it and is safe. —Proverbs 18:10

But the Lord is faithful, and He will strengthen and protect
you from the evil one. —2 Thessalonians. 3:3

. . . .

Provision
He who did not spare His own Son, but delivered Him
over for us all, how will He not also with Him freely give
us all things? —Romans 8:32

. . . .

Rest
Rest in the Lord and wait patiently for Him. —Psalm 37:7

Cease striving and know that I am God.— Psalm 46:10

"Come to Me, all who are weary and heavy-laden, and I will
give you rest. Take My yoke upon you and learn from Me, for
I am gentle and humble in heart, and you will find rest for
your souls. For My yoke is easy and My burden is light."
— Matthew 11:28–30

Let us be diligent to enter that rest. —Hebrews 4:11

. . . .

Salvation: By Faith in Christ
"For God so loved the world, that He gave His only
begotten Son, that whoever believes in Him shall
not perish, but have eternal life."— John 3:16

"I am the way, and the truth, and the life; no one comes to
the Father but through Me."— John 14:6

For I delivered to you as of first importance what I also received, that Christ died for our sins according to the Scriptures, and that He was buried, and that He was raised on the
third day according to the Scriptures. —1 Corinthians 15:3–4

For by grace you have been saved through faith; and that
not of yourselves, it is the gift of God; not as a result of
works, so that no one may boast. —EPHESIANS 2:8–9

. . . .

Security
He only is my rock and my salvation, my stronghold; I shall
not be shaken. On God my salvation and my glory rest; the
rock of my strength, my refuge is in God. —PSALM 62:6–7

"And I give eternal life to them, and they will never perish;
and no one will snatch them out of My hand. My Father, who
has given them to Me, is greater than all; and no one is able
to snatch them out of the Father's hand." —JOHN 10:28–29

. . . .

Sorrow
For His anger is but for a moment, His favor is for a lifetime;
weeping may last for the night, but a shout of joy comes in
the morning. —PSALM 30:5

. . . .

Sovereignty of God
"As for you, you meant evil against me, but God
meant it for good."—GENESIS 50:20

The counsel of the Lord stands forever, the plans of His
heart from generation to generation.—PSALM 33:11

His sovereignty rules over all. —PSALM 103:19b

But our God is in the heavens; He does whatever He pleases.
—PSALM 115:3

The Lord will accomplish what concerns me. —PSALM 138:8

Many are the plans in a man's heart, but the counsel of the
Lord will stand. —PROVERBS 19:21

"For the Lord of hosts has planned, and who
can frustrate it?" —ISAIAH 14:27

And we know that God causes all things to work together for good to those who love God, to those who are called according to His purpose. —ROMANS 8:28

[He] works all things after the counsel of His will. —EPHESIANS 1:11

. . . .

Steadfastness

I have set the Lord continually before me; because He is at my right hand, I will not be shaken. —PSALM 16:8

Therefore, my beloved brethren, be steadfast, immovable, always abounding in the work of the Lord, knowing that your toil is not in vain in the Lord. —1 Corinthians 15:58

. . . .

Strength

How blessed is the man whose strength is in You. . . . They go from strength to strength. —PSALM 84:5, 7

He gives strength to the weary, and to him who lacks might He increases power. . . . Yet those who wait for the Lord will gain new strength; they will mount up with wings like eagles, they will run and not get tired, they will walk and not become weary. —ISAIAH 40:29, 31

That He would grant you, according to the riches of His glory, to be strengthened with power through His Spirit in the inner man. —EPHESIANS 3:16

Be strong in the Lord and in the strength of His might. —EPHESIANS 6:10

I can do all things through Him who strengthens me. —PHILIPPIANS 4:13

Strengthened with all power, according to His glorious might, for the attaining of all steadfastness and patience; joyously giving thanks to the Father. —COLOSSIANS 1:11–12

. . . .

Suffering

For I consider that the sufferings of this present time
are not worthy to be compared with the glory that is
to be revealed to us. —ROMANS 8:18

For just as the sufferings of Christ are ours in abundance, so
also our comfort is abundant through Christ. —2 CORINTHIANS 1:5

Therefore we do not lose heart, but though our outer man is
decaying, yet our inner man is being renewed day by day. For
momentary, light affliction is producing for us an eternal
weight of glory far beyond all comparison, while we look not
at the things which are seen, but at the things which are not
seen; for the things which are seen are temporal, but the
things which are not seen are eternal. —2 CORINTHIANS 4:16–18

After you have suffered for a little while, the God of all grace,
who called you to His eternal glory in Christ, will Himself perfect, confirm, strengthen and establish you. —1 PETER 5:10

. . . .

Support

For the eyes of the Lord move to and fro throughout
the earth that He may strongly support those whose
heart is completely His. —2 CHRONICLES 16:9

. . . .

Temptation and Trials

No temptation has overtaken you but such as is common
to man; and God is faithful, who will not allow you to be
tempted beyond what you are able, but with the temptation
will provide the way of escape also, so that you will
be able to endure it. —1 CORINTHIANS 10:13

. . . .

Thoughts

For the mind set on the flesh is death, but the mind
set on the Spirit is life and peace. —ROMANS 8:6

We are taking every thought captive to the
obedience of Christ. —2 CORINTHIANS 10:5

Finally, brethren, whatever is true, whatever is honorable,
whatever is right, whatever is pure, whatever is lovely, whatever is of good repute, if there is any excellence and if anything worthy of praise, dwell on these things. —PHILIPPIANS 4:8

Therefore if you have been raised up with Christ, keep seeking the things above, where Christ is, seated at the right hand
of God. Set your mind on the things above, not on the things
that are on earth. For you have died and your life is hidden
with Christ in God. —COLOSSIANS 3:1–3

Therefore, prepare your minds for action, keep sober in spirit,
fix your hope completely on the grace to be brought to you at
the revelation of Jesus Christ. —1 PETER 1:13

. . . .

Trouble

For in the day of trouble He will conceal me in His tabernacle;
in the secret place of His tent He will hide me; He will
lift me up on a rock. —PSALM 27:5

In the day of my trouble I shall call upon You, for You
will answer me. —PSALM 86:7

. . . .

Trust

Trust in the Lord and do good; dwell in the land and cultivate
faithfulness. Delight yourself in the Lord; and He will give you
the desires of your heart. Commit your way to the Lord, trust
also in Him, and He will do it. —PSALM 37:3–5

In God I have put my trust, I shall not be afraid. What can
man do to me? —PSALM 56:11

Trust in the Lord with all your heart and do not lean on your
own understanding. In all your ways acknowledge Him, and
He will make your paths straight. —PROVERBS 3:5–6

. . . .

Victory

The Lord your God who goes before you will Himself fight on your behalf. —Deuteronomy 1:30

But thanks be to God, who always leads us in triumph in Christ, and manifests through us the sweet aroma of the knowledge of Him in every place. —2 Corinthians 2:14

For whatever is born of God overcomes the world; and this is the victory that has overcome the world—our faith.
—1 John 5:4

. . . .

Watchfulness of the Lord

Behold, the eye of the Lord is on those who fear Him, on those who hope for His lovingkindness. —Psalm 33:18

The eyes of the Lord are toward the righteous and His ears are open to their cry. —Psalm 34:15

. . . .

Weakness

My flesh and my heart may fail, but God is the strength of my heart and my portion forever. —Psalm 73:26

. . . .

Wisdom

Her ways are pleasant ways and all her paths are peace.
—Proverb 3:17

But the wisdom from above is first pure, then peaceable, gentle, reasonable, full of mercy and good fruits, unwavering, without hypocrisy. —James 3:17

. . . .

Word: Benefits of

Your word I have treasured in my heart, that I may not sin against You. —Psalm 119:11

If Your law had not been my delight, then I would have perished in my affliction. I will never forget Your precepts, for by them You have revived me. —PSALM 119:92–93

Your word is a lamp to my feet and a light to my path.
—PSALM 119:105

Those who love Your law have great peace, and nothing causes them to stumble. —PSALM 119:165

Your words were found and I ate them, and Your words became for me a joy and the delight of my heart; for I have been called by Your name, O Lord God of hosts.
—JEREMIAH 15:16

. . . .

The Word of God Endures

"Not one word of all the good words which the Lord your God spoke concerning you has failed." —JOSHUA 23:14b

"For truly I say to you, until heaven and earth pass away, not the smallest letter or stroke shall pass from the Law until all is accomplished." —MATTHEW 5:18

. . . .

Worry

"For this reason I say to you, do not be worried about your life, as to what you will eat or what you will drink; nor for your body, as to what you will put on. Is not life more than food, and the body more than clothing? Look at the birds of the air, that they do not sow, nor do they reap nor gather into barns, and yet your heavenly Father feeds them. Are you not worth much more than they? And who of you by being worried can add a single hour to his life? And why are you worried about clothing? Observe how the lilies of the field grow; they do not toil nor do they spin, yet I say to you that not even Solomon in all his glory clothed himself like one of these. But if God so clothes the grass of the field, which is alive today and tomorrow is thrown into the furnace, will He not much

more clothe you? You of little faith! Do not worry then,
saying, 'What will we eat?' or 'What will we drink?' or 'What
will we wear for clothing?' For the Gentiles eagerly seek all
these things; for your heavenly Father knows that you need
all these things. But seek first His kingdom and His
righteousness, and all these things will be added to you.
So do not worry about tomorrow; for tomorrow will care for
itself. Each day has enough trouble of its own."
—Matthew 6:25–34

Be anxious for nothing, but in everything by prayer and
supplication with thanksgiving let your requests be made
known to God. And the peace of God, which surpasses
all comprehension, will guard your hearts and your minds
in Christ Jesus. —Philippians 4:6–7

Casting all your anxiety on Him, because He cares for you.
—1 Peter 5:7

13

Everything
Does Happen
for a Reason

Everything happens for a reason? Yes. We may or may not see it, but the ultimate issue is that God is sovereign, He "works all things after the counsel of His will" (Eph. 1:11). God is in control. Absolutely and entirely.

Things do not happen at random. Man may plan and scheme, but God controls the outcome. "The counsel of the Lord stands forever, the plans of His heart from generation to generation" (Ps. 33:11). In fact, God "fashions the hearts of them all" (v. 15).

But God is never the author of evil. Man is always responsible for his sins, yet God's plan is never thwarted by man's folly. God's program will culminate the way God has determined it: "The Lord of hosts has planned, and who can frustrate it?" (Is. 14:27). No one. God says, "Even from eternity I am He, and there is none who can deliver out of My hand; I act and who can reverse it?" (Is. 43:13). No one. God is sovereign and in total control.

GOD IS SOVEREIGN

The Lord alone is God and He alone is sovereign. He declares, "I am God, and there is no other; I am God, and there is no one like Me, declaring the end from the beginning . . . saying, 'My purpose will be established, and I will accomplish all My good pleasure . . . I have planned it, surely I will do it'" (Isa. 46:9–11). Yes, "His sovereignty rules over all" (Ps. 103:19).

This truth is significant and ought to make us stop and reflect— seriously. Yes, difficult things—bad things—happen to us, yet God is sovereign and in control. What should that elicit from us? Faith. Trust. We are instructed: "Trust in the Lord with all your heart and do not lean on your own understanding. In all your ways acknowledge Him, and He will make your paths straight" (Prov. 3:5–6). We may not understand the "paths straight" that He makes in our lives, but in His sovereignty He does just that. There is a reason for everything that happens, whether or not we recognize it.

GOD IS LOVINGKINDNESS

But God's sovereignty is not understood in isolation. Alongside His sovereignty are His other attributes, and preeminent among those is His lovingkindness. The Psalms are replete with reminders of His lovingkindness. In the beloved Psalm 23 believers are reminded, "Surely goodness and lovingkindness will follow me all the days of my life." What a magnificent promise! "And I will dwell in the house of the Lord forever" (v. 6). David looked beyond this life when He would live with the Lord in glory forever. That was David's focus—and that should be our focus.

Did David have a difficult life? Yes, both before and after he became king. King Saul tried many times to kill David in anger and jealousy, beginning with a spear and ending with David being a man on the run, his life at risk (1 Sam. 19:9–11; 21–27; 29–30). Once king, his reign was marred by key sinful choices: his adultery with Bathsheba and the murder of Bathsheba's husband. The many consequences of those actions included the death of his child, the rebellion and conspiracy of his son Absalom, David's flight because of a conspiracy, Absalom's murder, and anarchy in his kingdom. Yet in the midst of all this trouble, David confessed his sins in public and in writing (see 2 Samuel 12:1–13 and Psalm 51). Ultimately good came as David turned to a wise, loving God, and King David could write, "All the paths of the Lord are lovingkindness and truth to those who keep His covenant and His testimonies" (Ps. 25:10).

David saw God in his suffering. He said, "I will rejoice and be glad in your lovingkindness, because You have seen my affliction; you have known the troubles of my soul" (Ps. 31:7). What did David do in his suffering? He recognized the lovingkindness of God. What an important lesson for us! And what was David's conclusion? "Be strong and let your heart take courage, all you who hope in the Lord" (Ps. 31:24).

EVERYTHING HAPPENS FOR A REASON

Ultimately, we must recognize that (1) God is sovereign and totally in control and (2) God is good, absolutely and entirely good. In His sovereignty and lovingkindness "God causes all things to work together for good to those who love God, to those who are called according to His purpose" (Rom. 8:28). Because God is sovereign and because God is good, everything that happens, happens for a reason. Our sovereign, good, and loving God is causing all things to cooperate (*sunergei*), to work together for the believers who, by His grace, He has called to Himself.

And what is the purpose of God bringing events into our lives and working them together for our good? It is that we "become conformed to the image of His Son" (Romans 8:29). Why do we have challenging illnesses, difficulties, and stress in life? So that we should learn to trust in God and not in ourselves; that we become conformed to the likeness of Christ.

In the sixteenth century, when Bible-believing ministers were punished by the Church of England, many being imprisoned for their faith (including John Bunyan), these men stood stalwart for their faith and wrote encouraging works that remain spiritually instructive for us today. In 1663 Thomas Watson wrote *All Things for Good*, in which Watson sees all events of life as happening for the believer's good. Despite enduring persecution by the Church of England, Watson could write, "There is more in the promises to comfort than in the world to perplex. . . . The mercies of God have a melting influence upon the soul; they dissolve it in the love of God. God's judgments make us fear Him; His mercies make us love Him."[1]

> God even brings about good through our sins, once we repent and return to Him.

Since God is sovereign and since He is also good, everything must happen for a reason. This has been discovered, and we have noted the enormous blessings that have resulted from severe suffering.

God even brings about good through our sins, once we repent and return to Him. Only eternity will reveal the changed lives through the ministry of Joni Eareckson Tada, a devout and brave warrior of the faith. Later in life Joni called the diving "accident" that left her a quadriplegic the best thing that ever happened to her, and she saw the love and goodness of God in the event. She believes that her accident came because of "the discipline of the Lord. . . . My diving accident was my heavenly Father's way of being a good daddy who needed to apply some reproof in my life, some correction . . . some discipline to get me back on the narrow way."

Joni has been paralyzed since age seventeen, but her words of faith and confidence may surprise you: "I couldn't be more pleased with God's decision; I couldn't be happier; and I say that even now—forty some odd years later—in this wheelchair!" Her ministry of comfort, challenge, and service has brought many to the Lord and has given consolation to those weakened by disease and disability.

"I [know] that my diving accident [has] changed things—it changed *everything!* It set me on a totally different path—and ultimately, it meant freedom and liberty as I reached out to Jesus for help and hope."[2]

Did Joni suffer? Immensely. Were people helped through her ministry? Countless numbers.

Likewise, David's sin with Bathsheba resulted in numerous bad things happening to the king of Israel—from loss of his child to anarchy in his kingdom—all because of sin. This is still true in the twenty-first century; people will suffer when they indulge in sin. Yet God was able to use David, who became a godly king influencing Israel to the good and who would remain "a man's after [God's] heart" (Acts 13:22; cf. 1 Sam.l 13:14).

AN AMAZING ANSWER

Normally we do not learn the answer to an injustice while in this world. Most of our answers will come in heaven. But on occasion God reveals His working. In China, some believers have answers to the tragic uprising in Tianamen Square more than twenty years ago. The Tianamen Square democracy movement in China in 1989 brought peaceful protests in schools and in Tianamen Square—and the wrath of the communist government, which squashed the uprising with troops and tanks. An estimated 2,600 Chinese people were killed by communist soldiers who attacked their own people. Where was God?

Chai Ling, a top leader in the protest movement, saw many friends die. She wondered about God and why He had permitted the triumph of evil forces. After she became a believer in Christ, she found the answer: "I see the country being transformed into a new nation. God used the massacre to pronounce the death of communism. We thought we were a political movement. What was really happening was a spiritual movement. God used the massacre to wake people up and prepare hearts and minds for a new spiritual awakening."[3]

Was there suffering and death? Yes, enormously so. Yet there was a reason—God was building His church in China. Today the Christian population of China probably exceeds one hundred million. Amid persecution and suffering, the church in China is growing.

FUTURE FOCUS

A significant problem for many of us is our focus on this life. When things fail in this life, we think all is lost. Our hope, our joy, our comfort seem entirely focused on this present world—and success in this world. *But we live in a fallen world.* Why do we think that life in this fallen world should be pristine, perfect, and eternally satisfying? It can't and it won't.

Our focus is wrong. We need to reflect on the words of Jesus, "He who loves his life loses it, and he who hates his life in this world will keep it to life eternal" (John 12:25). What is Jesus telling us? Is He expecting us to find our fulfillment in this life or in heaven? As Pastor Erwin Lutzer reminds us, "First the suffering, then the glory; first the cross, then the crown; first the pain, then the gain. . . . Suffering not only precedes glory, but suffering intensifies our desire for glory. . . . First comes Good Friday, then Resurrection Sunday."[4]

In our American materialism we—even as Christians—have inverted our value system. We think success and fulfillment belong in this life. We have failed to consider the life to come; we neglect to consider our future blessings in heaven. Yet the brevity of this life cannot compare with the joy and gladness of an eternal heaven.

Lutzer has wisely portrayed the prospect of eternity. He said that if we were to take a tape measure and cast it out to the farthest star, billions of light years away, eternity would only have begun. And our life on this earth would only be a hairline on the tape measure. Does that illustration help change our thinking?

"First the suffering, then the glory. First comes Good Friday, then Resurrection Sunday."

Our real citizenship is not in America; it is in heaven—we need to focus on where our real citizenship lies, "for our citizenship is in heaven, from which also we eagerly wait for a Savior, the Lord Jesus Christ" (Phil. 3:20). We are, in fact, already positionally seated in heaven and that is where we should keep our focus: "[God] raised us up with Him, and seated us with Him in the heavenly places in Christ Jesus" (Eph. 2:6). The triumphant return of Jesus Christ and our transformation is something we should constantly be anticipating (Titus 2:13). We need to be looking for our true country, our true homeland, like Abraham and the patriarchs (Heb. 11:14).

We also need to remember that our sufferings are *temporal*—our joy in heaven is *eternal*. And because of our future hope, we do not lose heart (2 Cor. 4:16–18).

The Final Chapter: Heaven

This present life is the final chapter on earth and the first chapter in heaven for every child of God. The ultimate event—death—is not a bad thing for God's people. D. L. Moody was right: When the believer's name is recorded in the obituary column, don't you believe it. Jesus spoke the climactic words in John 11:25–26: "I am the resurrection, and the life; he who believes in Me will live even if he dies, and everyone who lives and believes in Me will never die."

These words are entirely reliable and trustworthy. Their truthfulness is conditioned on the integrity of Jesus. Is Jesus reliable? Are His words trustworthy? Indeed they are. Then we can rest in the promises of John 11:25–26. He has assured us that even though we may die physically, we will live because He will resurrect our bodies. But He also reminds us there is a true sense in which we will never die. He said, "Everyone who lives and believes in Me shall never die." Spiritually, the believer will never die.

RESURRECTION BODIES

What kind of bodies will we have in heaven? The best explanation of our resurrection bodies is the resurrection body of Jesus Christ Himself. We can discover a great deal as we examine the resurrection accounts of our Lord. Jesus was recognizable in His resurrection body, indicating it was the same material body that He had during His earthly ministry. When Jesus spoke to Mary, she recognized Him (John 20:16). When the eyes of the disciples on the road to Emmaus were opened, they recognized the Savior (Luke 24:31). Jesus reminded the apostles that He was not simply a spirit; He had a body of flesh and bones (Luke 24:39). Moreover, the nail prints in His hands and the wound in His side revealed that His resurrection body had a continuity with His earthly body (John 20:20, 25). It was the same material body of His earthly life but it was glorified.

Unlike our earthly body that is perishable, our resurrection body will be imperishable (1 Cor. 15:42). This is significant. "Imperishable" (*aphtharsia*) means our resurrection body "is not subject to decay and control by sin."[1] This is the final resolution to our earthly struggles and sufferings. Think of it! No longer will we have any internal inclination to evil thoughts or actions. The capacity to sin will be gone. There will no longer be any suffering due to sin. But neither will our resurrection bodies be subject to decay. That means our glorified bodies will never entertain sickness, disease, or death. Our glorified bodies will be constant in health and vitality. What a prospect! *And that will continue for all eternity.*[2]

We cannot begin to compare the sufferings of the present with the glory of our future in heaven. They are beyond comparison. For this reason we should not lose hope. Paul reminds us, "Therefore we do not lose heart, but though our outer man is decaying, yet our inner man is being renewed day by day. For momentary, light affliction is producing for us an eternal weight of glory far beyond all comparison, while we look not at the things which are seen, but at the things which are not seen; for the things which are seen are temporal, but the things which are not seen are eternal" (2 Cor. 4:16–18).

Ultimately, our earthly sufferings must be weighed against heaven's glories. That will put the issues of life in perspective. Remember, we are eternal, and the drama of our earthly events must be evaluated alongside heaven's glories. Only then will we come to terms with the bad things of this life. Only then will we see that everything has a reason. In this context we are exhorted, "Therefore, my beloved brethren, be steadfast, immovable, always abounding in the work of the lord, knowing that your toil is not in vain in the Lord" (1 Cor. 15:58).

A TEENAGER ENTERS HEAVEN

Hildy was our cheerful, teenage neighbor girl. When our first son was young, Hildy would occasionally babysit for us. She was a reliable girl, mature beyond her middle-teen years, and a devout Christian. We could readily count on her; she had a strong Christian testimony.

But Hildy developed cancer, and one day as I returned home, I saw the big black car on the driveway of Hildy's home. It was a hearse. Hildy had died. A teenager at the threshhold of adulthood. Why would God take this vibrant, faithful teenager from her home and community? Wouldn't she have been useful for the Lord in His kingdom's work on earth? Couldn't she have served Him faithfully for many years?

Of course the answers remain locked up in the counsels of God. The finite cannot fathom the infinite. The sovereign God who makes no mistakes knows all the answers. Someday, in eternity, it may please Him to tell us—but then it probably won't matter.

I remember the funeral service. The pastor intoned Hildy's

exortation to her peers: "Tell the kids Jesus is real!" What a message! Hildy, a teenager, was dying and she knew it, but her faith was strong and she viewed life in the perspective of eternity. Jesus was what mattered, not the thrills of a temporary threescore and ten. Immortality was what mattered, not mortality.

DEATH IS GAIN

Paul's words, "For to me, to live is Christ, and to die is gain" (Phil. 1:21) were also Hildy's words. For her, living meant Christ. This life was wrapped up in Jesus Christ. The infinitive "to live" (*zein*) stresses the "act of living. . . . Living is coextensive with Christ."[3]

What a thought! For the believer, living involves a singular focus on Jesus Christ. "Life is summed up in Christ. Life is filled up with, occupied with Christ, in the sense that everything Paul does—trusts, loves, hopes, obeys, preaches, follows, and so on— is inspired by Christ and is done for Christ. Christ and Christ alone gives inspiration, direction, meaning, and purpose to existence. Paul views his life in time as totally determined and controlled by his own love for and commitment to Christ."[4]

But the other option—death—is not inferior. Paul says "to die is gain." "To die is gain" envisions the consequences of death. For the believer, death is profitable because it continues the life of fellowship with Christ. Moreover, we will see Christ in all His glory— the One who gave Himself for us.

THE GLORIES OF HEAVEN:
THE ULTIMATE RESOLUTION

The apostle John's vision of heaven remains a powerful description today:

> *Then I saw a new heaven and a new earth; for the first heaven and the first earth passed away, and there is no*

longer any sea. And I saw the holy city, new Jerusalem, coming down out of heaven from God, made ready as a bride adorned for her husband. And I heard a loud voice from the throne, saying, "Behold, the tabernacle of God is among men, and He will dwell among them, and they shall be His people, and God Himself will be among them, and He will wipe away every tear from their eyes; and there will no longer be any death; there will no longer be any mourning, or crying, or pain; the first things have passed away.

And He who sits on the throne said, 'Behold, I am making all things new.' And He said, "Write, for these words are faithful and true." (Rev. 21:1–5)

Who can fathom the wonder, the grandeur, the bliss of these words? Who can comprehend the peace, the comfort, the solace of heaven? The joy and glories of heaven are incomparable to anything in this life. Nor can the sufferings of this life be compared with the joy of heaven (see Romans 8:18). No matter how much we suffer or our loved ones suffer in this life, they are incomparable with the riches of the believer's inheritance in Christ.

Paul reminds us that since we are children of God, then we are "heirs also, heirs of God and fellow heirs with Christ, if indeed we suffer with Him so that we may also be glorified with Him" (Rom. 8:17). That's why Bible commentator James Stifler declared, "The intelligent believer does not hesitate to undergo sorrow in his service to Christ; he rather covets it in order that he may be glorified with Him; for the joint heirs are those who suffer that they may be glorified."[5] These promises are not those of a fairy tale; they are true. They are certain. Because of our mental limitations, it is we unbelieving humans who relegate these promises to some distant future. But that is not Paul's point. "What the Spirit of God would impress upon us is the certainty of the prospect. The glory is already existent and embodied in Christ. It is destined to be revealed to us at the return of Christ."[6]

We need to realize there is purpose in our suffering, whether or not we recognize it. The glories and blessings of heaven await us. Are our minds focused on heaven, or are they traumatized by suffering? Everything does happen for a good purpose.

Perhaps our mindset should be that of Habakkuk when he saw his world collapse:

> *I heard and my inward parts trembled . . . because I must wait quietly for the day of distress, for the people to arise who will invade us. Though the fig tree should not blossom and there be no fruit on the vines, though the yield of the olive should fail and the fields produce no food, though the flock should be cut off from the fold and there be no cattle in the stalls, yet I will exult in the Lord, I will rejoice in the God of my salvation. The Lord God is my strength, and He has made my feet like hinds' feet, and makes me walk on my high places." (Hab. 3:16–19)*

Amid the suffering we need to trust our heavenly Father and endure and persevere (James 1:3–4, 12).

My grandmother, who was twice widowed and who buried nine of her ten children, persevered. She trusted the sovereign, benevolent God even though she didn't understand. But her suffering was brief; she has entered heaven and is basking in the glories of heaven and reunion with her family—for all eternity. She persevered and "fought the good fight" As Paul exhorts us to do— and it was worth it. Everything has a reason with a sovereign God. Eternity will demonstrate that truth.

The issue is not whether we will suffer in this life. We will; everyone will. The singular issue is whether we will trust a sovereign God who is entirely good and causes all things to happen for a reason. Will I trust Him? Will you trust Him? God sent His

Son, Jesus Christ, to die on the cross as a substitute for our sins, so that we might be reconciled to a holy God. Having trusted Him, we can be assured of an *eternity* of heaven's glories that far surpass any suffering you and I will ever experience on this old earth.

Notes

Chapter 2: How Did Bad Things Begin?

1. "Who is Osama bin Laden?" *The St. Petersburg Times*, 13 September 2001, 26A.
2. Jamal Thalji, "Fallen Officer's Wife Recalls Last Goodbye," *The St. Petersburg Times*, 28 January 2001, 1.
3. Ibid.
4. Lilo T. Strauss et al., Surveillance Summary, 24 November 2006, vol. 55, no. 11, "Abortion Surveillance—United States, 2003"; accessed at http.//www.cdc.gov/mmwr/. From 1995–2003 the abortion rate was 900,000 lives annually.
5. "Early Gift Helps Famine-Stricken Ethiopia," *Florida Baptist Witness*, 4 May 2000, 1.
6. "Somalia Famine: UN Warns of 750,000 Deaths," BBC Mobile, 5 September 2011, http.//www.bbc.co.uk/news/world-africa-14785304.
7. "December 2000 Tuscaloosa Tornado," at http://en.wikipedia.org/wiki/December_2000_Tuscaloosa_tornado.
8. "Girl Survives Twister; Dad, Brother Killed," *The Tampa Tribune*, 19 December 2000, 6 N/W.

Chapter 3: Is God in Control?

1. Harold S. Kushner, *When Bad Things Happen to Good People* (New York: Avon Books, 1981), 14.
2. Ibid., 46.
3. Ibid., 53, 55.
4. Ibid., 127, 129.
5. F. F. Bruce, *The Epistles to the Colossians to Philemon and to the Ephesians* in The New International Commentary on the New Testament (Grand Rapids: Eerdmans, 1984), 263–264.
6. Several writers have discussed antinomies. See J. I. Packer, *Evangelism and the Sovereignty of God* (Downers Grove, IL: InterVarsity, 1967) and Kenneth Boa, *God, I Don't Understand* (Colorado Springs: Victor, 2007).
7. See Fritz Rienecker and Cleon Rogers Jr., *The Linguistic Key to the Greek*

New Testament (Grand Rapids: Zondervan, 1982), 308.

8. I heard the story of God's great provision for Word of Life in Hungary while teaching classes at the Toalmas Word of Life Institute in 1996, 1998, and 2000.

9. Karen Giesen, "Prof, n." *Kindred Spirit*, 24:2 (Summer 2000), 5; also at http://www.dts.edu/publications/read/prof-n-karen-giesen/.

10. "Hurricane Andrew Facts" at www.tropicalweather.net. In 2005 Hurricane Katrina would become the costliest in terms of total damage at $80 billion (see "Hurricane Katrina Facts" at www.tropicalweather.net).

11. Lynn Vincent, "Long Road Ahead," *World*, 16 September 2000, 25.

12. Ibid.

Chapter 4: Is God Sovereign over Evil?

1. Corrie ten Boom, Elizabeth Sherrill, and John Sherrill, *The Hiding Place* (Old Tappan, NJ: Revell, 1971), 197.

2. Corrie ten Boom with Jamie Buckingham, *Tramp for the Lord* (Old Tappan, NJ: Revell,1974), 55–57.

3. Alan F. Johnson, *Romans*, vol. 2 (Chicago: Moody, 1985), 33.

4. *St. Petersburg Times*, 26 December 1989, 2A.

5. *World*, 7 May 2011, 48.

6. Ibid.

7. Ibid.

8. Gerald F. Hawthorne, *Philippians* in Word Biblical Commentary (Waco, TX: Word, 1983), 60.

9. Kenneth S. Wuest, *Philippians in the Greek New Testament* (Grand Rapids: Eerdmans, 1942), 54.

10. Charles Hodge, *The Second Epistle to the Corinthians* (London: Banner of Truth Trust, 1959 reprint), 10.

Chapter 5: How Powerful Is Satan?

1. F. Delitzsch, *Biblical Commentary on the Book of Job* (Grand Rapids: Eerdmans, 1970 reprint), 1:68.

2. Roy B. Zuck, "Job," in *The Bible Knowledge Commentary: Old Testament* (Wheaton: Victor, 1985), 721.

3. Cleon L. Rogers Jr. and Cleon L. Rogers III, *The New Linguistic and Exegetical Key to the Greek New Testament* (Grand Rapids: Zondervan, 1998), 475.

4. C. Fred Dickason, *Angels: Elect & Evil*, rev. ed. (Chicago: Moody, 1995), 153–54.

5. Ibid., 154.

6. *Florida Baptist Witness*, 26 August 2010, 12.

Notes

7. Ibid.

8. See *The Agony of Deceit*, Michael Horton, ed. (Chicago: Moody, 1990); D. R. McConnell, *A Different Gospel* (Peabody, MA: Hendrickson, 1988); and Bruce Barron, *The Health and Wealth Gospel* (Downers Grove, IL: InterVarsity, 1987).

9. Wilhelm Michaelis, "Methodeia," *Theological Dictionary of the New Testament*, trans. Geoffrey W. Bromiley, (Grand Rapids: Eerdmans, 1967), 5:102–103.

10. D. Edmond Hiebert, *The Thessalonian Epistles* (Chicago: Moody, 1971), 142.

11. William F. Arndt, F. Wilbur Gingrich, and Frederick W. Danker *A Greek-English Lexicon of the New Testament*, 2nd ed. (Chicago: Univ. of Chicago, 1979), 868.

12. Hiebert, *The Thessalonian Epistles*, 334.

13. Ibid., 333–34.

14. See discussion, Stephen S. Smalley, *1, 2, 3 John* in Word Biblical Commentary (Waco, TX: Word, 1984), 303. Among those holding this view are B. F. Westcott, A. E. Brooke, C. H. Dodd, and W. E. Vine.

15. Rogers Jr. and Rogers III, *The New Linguistic and Exegetical Key*, 599.

16. Randy Alcorn, *If God Is Good* (Colorado Springs: Multnomah, 2009), 51; as cited in David Jeremiah, *I Never Thought I'd See the Day!* (New York, Faith Words, 2011), 58.

17. Jeremiah, *I Never Thought I'd See the Day!*, 58.

Chapter 6: How Does Sin Affect Our Suffering?

1. As quoted in *Growing Your Church through Training and Motivation*, Marshall Shelley, ed. (Minneapolis: Bethany, 1997), n.p.

2. Robert G. Gromacki, *Called to Be Saints* (Grand Rapids: Baker, 1977), 84.

3. Charles Hodge, *The First Epistle to the Corinthians* (London: Banner of Truth Trust, 1958 reprint), 106.

4. "Study: Being Overweight, Not Just Obese, Raises Death Rate"; *USA Today*, 1 December 2010; www.usatoday.com/yourlife/fitness/2010-12-01-overweight-death_n.htm.

5. Richard J. Wagman, *The New Complete Medical and Health Encyclopedia* (Chicago: Ferguson, 1977), 2:398.

6. As quoted in John Piper, *God's Passion for His Glory* (Wheaton: Crossway, 1998), 32.

7. Howard G. Hendricks, "Training Children in the Way They Should Grow," *Good News Broadcaster*, April 1973, 18.

8. *St. Petersburg Times*, 22 April 2000, 10A.

9. Cleon L. Rogers Jr. and Cleon L. Rogers III, *The New Linguistic and Exegetical Key to the Greek New Testament* (Grand Rapids: Zondervan, 1998), 446.

10. Horst Balz and Gerhard Schneider, eds., *Exegetical Dictionary of the New Testament*, 3 vols. (Grand Rapids: Eerdmans, 1993), 3:3.

11. Rogers Jr. and Rogers III, *The New Linguistic and Exegetical Key*, 446.

12. F. F. Bruce, *The Epistles to the Colossians, to Philemon, and to the Ephesians* (Grand Rapids: Eerdmans, 1984), 134.

Chapter 7: Why Are God's People Persecuted?

1. Obed Minchakpu, "Moving Toward War?" *Christianity Today*, 24 April 2000, 29.

2. Franklin Graham, "Stand Up for Sudan's Christians," *The Wall Street Journal*, 15 March 2000.

3. *Christianity Today*, 10 July 2000, 27.

4. M. Smith, "Mission into the Unknown," *National Liberty Journal*, vol. 29, no. 7, 1.

5. Ibid., 3.

6. Michael Ireland, "Closure for Three Kidnapped New Tribes Missionaries," Assist News Service, 13 November 2001, http://www. assistnews.net/strategic/s0111037.htm; Deann Alford, "New Tribes Missionaries Kidnapped in 1993 Declared Dead," 1 September 2001, *Christianity Today*, http://www.christianitytoday.com/ct/2001/septemberweb-only/9-24-44.0.html.

7. C. Henry Smith and Cornelius Krahn, *The Story of the Mennonites*, 4th ed. (Newton, KS: Mennonite Publication Office, 1957), 116.

8. For more on the five missionaries and the impact of their martyrdom, see Paul Robertson and James Vincent, *A Vision with Wings* (Chicago: Moody 1992), 88–90.

9. See Jim Elliot, *The Journals of Jim Elliot*, rev. ed., Elisabeth Elliot, ed. (Grand Rapids: Revell, 1978), 28 October 1949 entry. The *Life* magazine account appears in "Go Ye and Preach the Gospel. Five Do and Die," *Life*, 30 January 1956.

10. Elisabeth Elliot, *Through Gates of Splendor* (Old Tappan, NJ: Revell, 1957), 201–202].

11. Elisabeth Elliot, *The Savage My Kinsman* (Ann Arbor, MI: Servant, 1996), cf. p. 151.

12. Ibid., 152.

13. A. Thompson, *The Book of Jeremiah* in The International Commentary on the Old Testament (Grand Rapids: Eerdmans, 1980), 396.

14. D. Edmond Hiebert, *The Thessalonian Epistles* (Chicago: Moody, 1971), 60.

15. William F. Arndt, F. Wilbur Gingrich, and Frederick W. Danker, *A Greek-English Lexicon of the New Testament*, 2nd ed., (Chicago: Univ. of Chicago, 1979), 362.

16. Hiebert, *The Thessalonian Epistles*, 59.

17. C. K. Barrett, *A Commentary on the Epistle to the Romans* (New York: Harper & Row, 1957), 103.

18. Ibid.

19. Douglas Moo, *The Epistle to the Romans* (Grand Rapids: Eerdmans, 1996), 302.

20. See Carl Moeller and David W. Hegg with Craig Hodgkins, *The Privilege of Persecution* (Chicago: Moody, 2011), especially ch. 5; Paul Marshall with Lela Gilbert, *Their Blood Cries Out* (Waco, TX: Word, 1997); and Nina Shea, *In the Lion's Den* (Nashville: Broadman & Holman, 1997).

21. F. F. Bruce, *The Book of Acts* in The New International Commentary on the New Testament (Grand Rapids: Eerdmans, 1954), 336.

22. His interactions have been relayed through the *Washington Post*, CNN, and *Time* magazine, among others. For a profile of Dr. Mohler and his interactions with the media on public issues, see the cover story by Molly Worthen, "The Reformer," *Christianity Today*, October 2010.

Chapter 8: Why Suffer for the Gospel?

1. The Associated Press, "Lone Survivor Details Massacre," *The Tampa Tribune*, 12 August 2010.

2. "Volunteers Mourned," *The Tampa Tribune*, 9 August 2010, 8.

3. Susan Estrich, "Tebows' Abortion Deception," *St. Petersburg Times*, 28 January 2010, 13A.

4. Ibid.

5. Cleon L. Rogers Jr. and Cleon L. Rogers III, *The New Linguistic and Exegetical Key to the Greek New Testament* (Grand Rapids: Zondervan, 1998), 453.

6. Ibid., 454.

7. Ibid., 399.

8. The information about William Carey is taken from George Smith, *Life of William Carey*, 1922 reprint.

9. W. E. Vine, *The Epistles to Timothy and Titus* (London: Oliphants, 1965), 145.

Chapter 9: What's the Purpose of Suffering?

1. Cleon L. Rogers Jr. and Cleon L. Rogers III, *The New Linguistic and Exegetical Key to the Greek New Testament* (Grand Rapids: Zondervan, 1998), 324.

2. C. K. Barrett, *The Epistle to the Romans* (New York: Harper & Row, 1957), 103.

3. Nonetheless, Douglas Moo says, "We are to exult 'in' the afflictions themselves; that is, to view them as a basis for further confidence in our redeemed status," in *The Epistle to the Romans* in The New International Commentary on the New Testament (Grand Rapids: Eerdmans, 1996), 302. C. E. B. Cranfield says, "We actually exult in tribulations. . . . Afflictions are actually cause for exultation" *Romans: A Shorter Commentary* (Grand Rapids: Eerdmans, 1985), 104.

4. Rogers Jr. and Rogers III, *The New Linguistic and Exegetical Key*, 324.

5. All information from "Dave Dravecky: 'Comeback,'" American Tract Society, adapted from Dave Dravecky, *Comeback* (Grand Rapids: Zondervan, 1990).

6. Ibid.

7. Rogers Jr. and Rogers III, *The New Linguistic and Exegetical Key,* 324; William F. Arndt, F. Wilbur Gingrich, and Frederick W. Danker *A Greek-English Lexicon of the New Testament*, 2nd ed. (Chicago: Univ. of Chicago, 1979), 202.

8. Alan F. Johnson, *Romans: The Freedom Letter*, vol. 1, rev. ed. (Chicago: Moody, 1984), 87.

9. Gingrich and Danker, *Greek-English Lexicon*, 252–53.

10. Information taken from a lecture given by Afshin Ziafat at Idlewild Baptist Church, Tampa, Florida, 1 March 2001; and Randy Bonser, "When Embracing Your Father Means Losing Your Dad," *Believe*, August 2000, 14–17.

11. Robert J. Morgan, "It Is Well with My Soul," in *Then Sings My Soul* (Nashville: Nelson, 2003), 185; Kenneth W. Osbeck, *101 Hymn Stories* (Grand Rapids: Kregel, 1982), 126–27.

12. Ibid.

Chapter 10: How Our Loss Can Benefit Others

1. Personal conversations with Chris and Samantha Conti at Southeast Baptist Seminary, Wake Forest, South Carolina, in 2001.

2. Erwin Lutzer, *One Minute After You Die* (Chicago: Moody, 1997), 126–27.

3. Toby Willis, "Why Do Bad Things Happen to Good People?" Gospel tract (no publisher).

4. Cleon L. Rogers Jr. and Cleon L. Rogers III, *The New Linguistic and Exegetical Key to the Greek New Testament* (Grand Rapids: Zondervan, 1998), 392.

5. Ibid., 564.

6. Horatio G. Spafford, "It Is Well with My Soul." In public domain. In verse 3 Spafford wrote that His sin "is nailed to the cross and I bear it no more." His response is to declare, "Praise the Lord, praise the Lord, O my soul!"

7. Robert J. Morgan, *Then Sings My Soul* (Nashville: Nelson, 2003), 205; see also "Darlene Deibler Rose—Prisoner of War" at http://www.johndubler.comDarlene_Deibler_Rose_Part_II.pdf for more on Darlene's life and testimony while in the Kampili prison camp.

8. Jon Anderson, "Camera Captured Hoover Man's Fight with Tumor," *Birmingham News*, 27 September 2000.

9. Ibid.

10. Rogers Jr. and Rogers III, *The New Linguistic and Exegetical Key*, 392.

11. W. Radl, "Hupomone," *Exegetical Dictionary of the New Testament*, Horst Balz and Gerhard Schneider, eds., (Grand Rapids: Eerdmans 1993), 3:406.

12. Edna J. Rogers, "Yea, Though I Walk through the Valley," pamphlet, 31 May 2003.

13. Ibid.

Chapter 11: The Ultimate Resolution

1. Read the entire story in Paul Bubar, *Not by Chance* (Delmar, NY: First Century, 2003).

2. M. Bergeron, Sound of Grace, ic@mdc.net.

3. Writer unknown, "This World Is Not My Home"; apparently first published in *Joyful Meeting in Glory*, No. 1, Bertha Davis, ed. (Sterling, KY: Miller, 1919).

4. W. R. Moody, *The Life of Dwight L. Moody* (Westwood, NJ: Barbour and Co., 1985 reprint), 467 ff.

5. Ibid.

6. Fritz Rienecker, *A Linguistic Key to the Greek New Testament*, Cleon L. Rogers Jr., ed. (Grand Rapids: Zondervan, 1980), 638.

Chapter 13: Everything *Does* Happen for a Reason

1. Thomas Watson, *All Things for Good* (Edinburgh: Banner of Truth, 1986), 17–18.

2. Joni Eareckson Tada, "Sin and Suffering," *Joni and Friends*, 10 June 2011.

3. Timothy C. Morgan, "Saving China's Daughters," *Christianity Today*, October 2011, 35.

4. Erwin W. Lutzer, *The Vanishing Power of Death* (Chicago: Moody, 2004), 56, 58.

The Final Chapter: Heaven

1. Cleon L. Rogers Jr. and Cleon L. Rogers III, *The New Linguistic and Exegetical Key to the Greek New Testament* (Grand Rapids: Zondervan, 1998), 388.

2. For more information on our heavenly body and our relationships in heaven, see Paul Enns, *Heaven Revealed* (Chicago: Moody, 2010), chap. 5 and 12.

3. A. T. Robertson, *Word Pictures in the New Testament* (Nashville: Broadman, 1931), 4:441.

4. Gerald F. Hawthorne, *Philippians* in Word Biblical Commentary (Waco, TX: Word, 1983), 45.

5. James M. Stifler, *The Epistle to the Romans* (Chicago: Moody, 1960), 143.

6. W. E. Vine, *The Epistle to the Romans* (Grand Rapids: Zondervan, 1948), 123.

HEAVEN REVEALED

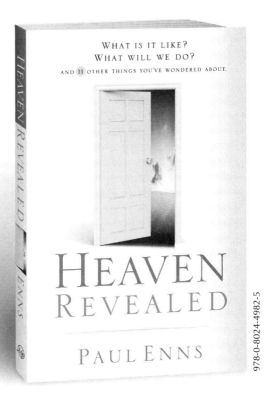

In grief, we all need hope—hope for our loved ones who are now gone, and hope for ourselves as eternity looms closer. Paul Enns takes us through what the Bible has to say about heaven in a clear and personal manner so that we are left with no confusion, only the hope that we so desire.

Also available as an ebook

www.MoodyPublishers.com

THE MOODY HANDBOOK
OF THEOLOGY

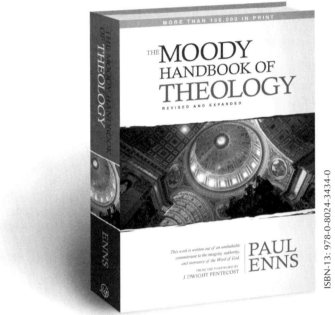

ISBN-13: 978-0-8024-3434-0

The Moody Handbook of Theology leads the reader into the appreciation and understanding of the essentials of Christian theology. It introduces the reader to the five dimensions that provide a comprehensive view of theology: biblical theology, systematic theology, historical theology, dogmatic theology, and contemporary theology. Paul Enns provides a concise doctrinal reference tool for newcomer and scholar. Includes new material on the openness of God, health and wealth theology, the emergent church, various rapture interpretations, feminism, and more.

Also available as an ebook

MoodyPublishers.com